Also by KEN BUMPUS:

"Those Crazy Camera Guys"

ISBN 978-1-4669-0623-5 (sc)
ISBN 978-1-4669-0622-8 (e)

Published 2011 by:
Trafford Publishing Co.
1663 Liberty Drive
Bloomington, IN 47403

Cover Photo: The author in Vung Tao awaiting transport to his next assignment in VIETNAM

NAVY PHOTOGRAPHERS

IN

VIETNAM

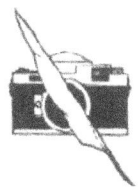

**Combat Camera Group Team <u>Alfa-Two</u>
takes over the mission.**
A sequel to "Those Crazy Camera Guys"

Ken Bumpus

Order this book online at www.trafford.com
or email orders@trafford.com

Most Trafford titles are also available at major online book retailers.

Printed in the United States of America.

ISBN: 978-1-4669-3006-3 (sc)
ISBN: 978-1-4669-3005-6 (e)

Trafford rev. 05/04/2012

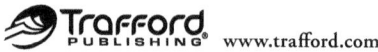 www.trafford.com

North America & international
toll-free: 1 888 232 4444 (USA & Canada)
phone: 250 383 6864 ♦ fax: 812 355 4082

— PREVIEW —

Navy Chief Photographer's Mate Timothy 'Gung-Ho'
Gilmore leads a five-man team of specially trained documentary
photographers and journalists on missions throughout
Vietnam recording Navy and Marine actions.

From the swamps of the southern Delta to the DMZ
in the north, Gilmore and his men send back to
Washington the pictures (movie and still), showing the
citizens 'back home' what this "war" is all about.

To keep their sanity in this insane environment, they cope
with humor and light-hearted banter in their off-duty lives

Dedicated to my daughter BETH, my grandson RYAN
and, with THANKS, to all my Shipmates and Friends who enjoyed
(or not) my first compilation of the antics of a ficticious group of
Navy Combat Photographers depicted in "Those Crazy Camera
Guys". I thank you for your encouragement and being 'on my six'.
I couldn't have done it without you.

I SALUTE YOU WITH MY WORDS,

BUT THE MOST SINCERE ARE THESE:

"May you always enjoy

FAIR WINDS AND FOLLOWING SEAS" *

* *Traditional NAVY farewell*

ONE

The Pan-Am aircraft carrying Senior Chief Brady and his Combat Camera Group, Detachment <u>ALPHA ONE</u> team on their journey home had barely cleared Vietnam air space, before his relief—Chief Photographer's Mate Timothy ('Gung Ho') Gilmore—had his CCG <u>ALPHA-TWO</u> team 'turnin'-and-a-burnin'.

They piled into the van with all their photo gear and went whizzing along to their office on Tan Son Nhut Air Base.

"OK, we have one hour to get all this gear inventoried and stowed away shipshape and then we'll get the 'skinny' from Ensign Duncan. With any luck we just may be hittin' the jungle trail real soon. I can't wait to get one of those yellow slope-heads in my sights."

"Hey, Chief, we're supposed to be over here to shoot pictures, NOT gooks." Second Class Photographers Mate 'Louie' Lucase hollered from the rear of the van.

"Louie, I fully intend to do a LOT of both ! Now, you muttenheads we're here and it's time to get this gear inside and on the shelves, PRONTO!"

Louie is a 24-year-old Cajun from the bayou country of Louisiana. He ran away to New Orleans at the age of 12 and grew up in the French Quarter 'swamping out' the Bourbon Street clubs just to be around his idols, the greats of Dixieland Jazz.

After years of trying, he still has not mastered any musical instrument. His idols were blunt in telling him that he had a 'tin ear'. Undeterred, he still lugs around a beat-up old clarinet wherever his Navy assignments take him and leaves behind a large group of howling dogs and suffering music lovers. With each failed attempt to coax the right sound out of the instrument, 'Louie' grows more and more frustrated.

His main talent, however, is 'scrounging'. If the unit needs anything not supplied through Navy channels, 'Louie' can 'beg, borrow, or misappropriate' it—or even, <u>make it</u>. His mechanical abilities are unlimited. In high school shop class he had constructed a tripod for his Arriflex movie camera that is the envy of all his photo buddies. With tubing and junked aircraft parts, he had constructed one of the lightest, smoothest operating and steadiest camera stands in existence.

"Give me 'Duck Tape' and a can of WD-40 and I can fix anything," 'Louie' claimed.

The three other team members, are not without their specialized talents.

Photographers Mate Second Class Dennis 'Baldy' Baldwin didn't get his nickname from his last name nor for his lack of hair. On the contrary, His fast-growing, jet-black hair almost shrouds his body making him resemble a gorilla in the morning, before shaving—which he has to do twice a day to remain presentable in public.

In 'boot' camp 'Baldy' was forced to go to the barber every three or four days until he hit on his only solution—get a 'burr-cut'—clippers all over, leaving about 1/8 inch of stubble.—hence his nickname. It also made grooming much simpler in the muggy Vietnam climate.

"Just start washing your face and don't stop 'til you reach your collar," claims 'Baldy'.

He came from International Falls, Minnesota, "the coldest f——king place this side of either Pole." He relishes the heat of Southeast Asia.

His other outstanding talent is with a movie camera. He brags that he is 'The Rembrandt of the Arriflex'. His camera is 'his brush, the film his canvas'. He sleeps with his camera within arms'-reach alongside his tripod and .45.

Journalist Second Class Seth Pinkney, at 29, is the oldest of the team (excepting Chief Gilmore), and hails from Back Bay, Boston.

He's the quiet, studious type. He was attending Harvard studying fine art but, in his junior year, he got involved in a melee in Boston's 'red-light' district, (a not too reputable section)—"just an observer, not a participant". Harvard did not look on the incident favorably.

"You had no right being there. It's 'out of bounds' to undergrads."

So they booted him. No longer a student, he was about to be drafted, so he enlisted in the Navy. Because of his education he was offered OCS (Officers' Candidate School) but opted, instead, to accept a Petty Officer Second Class rating in journalism. It suited him fine and, after 'boot' camp, he was selected to attend the Navy-sponsored one-year course in photojournalism at Syracuse University.

On graduating, his first duty assignment was to Pacific Fleet Combat Camera Group, in San Diego. Before he had time to get accustomed to his new location, he was ordered to SERE School (Survival-Evasion-Resistance and Escape) in the desert of California. From there he spent two weeks in Marine Camp Pendleton undergoing small-arms training. When he had finished this preparation for combat, he was shipped off to Yokosuka, Japan to join CCG team ALPHA TWO—just as they were packing to head for Saigon to relieve Senior Chief Brady's ALPHA ONE team !

"Roger the Dodger" Simpson rounds out the roster. He's a Third Class Photographer's Mate from a suburb of Detroit. Before entering the Navy he had been a promising pro-ball player, headed for the minor leagues. An injured elbow halted his pitching career and his dream. His interest in photography led him to open a commercial photo business. Roger soon found out 'business sense' does not necessarily go along with good 'photo sense', so he closed up shop and signed up to beat the draft. He is a 'switch hitter' photographer—talented in still, as well as mopic photography.

He loves the monsoon rains, and getting soaked standing in the downpour. Roger swears it soothes his aching arm.

Last, but not least, is the team leader. Chief Timothy "Gung Ho" Gilmore. He served in the Korean 'police action' and spent several months in a POW camp, suffering the beatings and bouts with numerous diseases. While being moved to a different camp, he and another prisoner escaped by overpowering their two guards and disposing of them with bamboo spikes. They survived in the woods and mountains of North Korea until linking-up with a squad of Marines making their withdrawal (NOT RETREATING !) from the Chosen Reservoir.

He lost friends in Korea and swore "those little yellow bastards will pay for those men, some day, and I want to be there to collect."

The Chief retired after Korea but, when Vietnam flared up, he immediately volunteered to return to active duty—"so I can kicked some more yellow Commies' butts."

The teams' only worry is that, given the chance, he'll lead them across the DMZ (the Demilitarized Zone) dividing North and South Vietnam right into Hanoi.

The stowing job was finished just as Ensign Duncan walked in.

"Glad to see you're all here 'cause I have important news. This is HIGHEST SECURITY Info so keep your lips zipped, SAVVY ? Things are 'heating up near a place called Pleiku and CHINFO (Chief of Naval Information) wants us to give the Marines saturation coverage. Now I don't need to tell you, but this'll be a 'hairy' one. Not all of you can go so you can draw straws. The two long ones go. OK ?"

"I damn sure better get a long one. I'm ready to mix it up with those slimy bastards," growled Chief Gilmore.

"Don't worry, Chief, if you miss this one, you'll get plenty of chances later," replied Ensign Duncan. "I understand from Pac Fleet intel, that there are going to be tac son (many) big pushes coming up."

"That's GREAT with me. The more the merrier !"

The conversation was buzzing when 'Teach' entered.

"I guess you guys must have gotten some good news, from all the chatter. Well I have some more for you." said 'Teach', flashing a mile-wide grin.

"Ensign Duncan, you'd best get into the proper uniform-of-the-day. I was just over at Seventh Fleet Detachment Office, and they informed they had just received word from DC. You are no longer an Ensign in this here canoe club. Effective immediately, you've been promoted to Lieutenant Junior Grade ! So get the silver bars on your collar before you get 'written up' for being out of uiform."

A window-shattering HOORAH ! went up from the troops and everyone was pushing and shoving to shake the officer's hand and slap him on the back (the first and last time that would be allowed).

"Men, I just want to say—this is a humungous honor, and I owe it all to you guys and Senior Chief Brady's crew. You guys have always made me 'look good'—despite all your shenanigans.—THANKS !

"Now, let's get at this straw-drawing game. Long ones go to Pleiku and what fate will follow, The rest of you sh—t birds can hit the club for ONE HOUR, then it's back to our Saigon Villa to prepare for whatever tomorrow may throw our way.

"I'll hold the straws. Line up and make your choice. Hold your straws until all of you have picked, then show them altogether. Junior man first. Roger, step up."

In ascending order, each man drew a straw. When they revealed their straws, the lucky (??) two men holding the long ones were 'Louie' and the chief.

'OK, Chief, listen up and I'll lay it out for you. You'll both carry still and mopic gear and go armed—you'll be expected to do your photography as well as 'engage' the VC when necessary.

"A couple months ago the VC infiltrated our defenses at the airbase near Pleiku and hit them with 'satchel' charges, mortars and captured US howitzers.

"The casualties were extensive. Now, we're sending in a 'search and destroy' mission to root them out of their jungle strongholds. You two will accompany a large force of battle-hardened US Marines and ARVN (South Vietnamese) Special Forces. They're going in on four UH-1B Helos. They'll set down on a LZ (landing zone) about 5 clicks (km) south of the VC enclave.

"We're hoping to catch them off guard, and get you on the ground before they know you're there. Surprise is essential, so mum's the word."

"Lieutenant, those helos will be sitting ducks if the VC get wind that we're coming. I sure hope those monkeys never duck hunted and know how to 'lead the bird', like we learned back in Minnesota," commented 'Baldy'.

"I'll second that," replied Louie. "I got tak son women yet to be wooed."

"You and 'your women', Louie. You haven't had such good luck with them in the past—two marriages down the drain," remarked 'Teach'.

"To set the record straight, Teach. I wasn't to blame in either case. When I met the first one I was sure I'd found 'Mrs. Right', but after marriage I quickly found out her first name turned out to be **ALWAYS!** The second one left me for a trumpet-player from Bourbon Street and I think, to this day, it was because of the way he held his lips !"

"Let's get serious, now, Guys. Chief, you'll catch an 'Air America' (CIA undercover airline) Beechcraft on the flight line at 1300 (1 pm)," Mr. Duncan instructed.

"They'll fly you to Plieku where the helos will be waiting to load up with you and the Marines and ARVN for a dawn takeoff. Each of you pile on separate 'birds' and take your marching orders from the ranking Marine aboard. It's going to be crowded so 'hit the dirt' running—just like you were trained to do back at Ream Field in 'Diego.—I warn you, CYA (cover your asses)!"

The flight to Plieku went without a hitch, but shortly after disembarking, 'Louie' was confronted by a 'Shavetail' Marine Second Lieutenant who began berating him for FAILING TO SALUTE! This, from a man just arrived 'in country' and whose boots were still unscuffed and free of any Plieku dust.

'Louie' was flabbergasted and just stood at attention smiling. The louder the Marine hollered, the wider 'Louie's' smile, which only further enraged the young officer. Finally, thoroughly disgusted, he stormed off.

"Jeeze, 'Louie', I thought for a minute he was going to hit you," Chief Gilmore whispered. *"What were you thinking, just standing there smiling, while he chewed your ass?"*

"Well, Chief, I learned, long ago, while they're laying it on, smiling just drives them NUTS!"

"It worked—this time, but be careful—some officers might have you slapped into the BRIG for insubordination!"

"Can't help it, Chief. It's just my natural reaction."

The word was passed along—*"Briefing for all pilots, squad leaders and attached personnel in fifteen minutes in the Operations tent."*

"I guess you know, Louie, 'attached personnel' means us," Gilmore said. "We photogs and news media have a $5000 bounty on our heads, so we don't advertise our presence if we know what's good for us.

"Come on, lets go get the latest scoop. We don't want to find out the plan after we're already facing 'Charlie.'"

The Marine Lt Col. began by informing them "The LZ (landing zone) that has been picked for this 'set-down', has suddenly become 'home' for a flock birds. This means that you pilots are going to find a crowded airspace. *'Yellow-tail Leader'* I'd suggest you make a low-altitude, high-speed run over the LZ to scatter the birds, and you other pilots follow as close as is safe, drop your troops, and di-di Mao out of there before the VC can react. You'll be coming in just before sun-up so use that to your advantage and approach low, from the east, that'll put the sun at your back and the VC will have to be looking right into it.

"All you squad leaders have your maps with the grids marked out on them, and, from available intel, the locations of your targets. Any questions?

"OK. Reveille is at 0400, 'wheels up' at 0500. Good hunting, men. Let's 'grease' those 'dinks'!"

With the air filled with the before-battle tension, Chief Gilmore and 'Louie' slept fitfully and sprang out of bed at 0400, wolfed down the Marine breakfast and were rarin' to go long before time to board their 'choppers'.

"Louie, I'll ride in the lead chopper. You catch number three," the Chief instructed. "Stick with your men like glue. Try to get some air-to-air shots of the other helos and, if possible, some close-ups of faces of your guys. Take care ! I'll see you back in Pleiku when this is over. **God willing !"**

"Chief, you be careful, too. I know how you acquired the "Gung Ho" name and want to 'get even', but don't get reckless. The Navy needs you."

Two

Five AM came and the four UH-1B birds went airborne.

Approaching the LZ, it was obvious the flock of birds were in control of the pad. The pilot of *'Yellow-Tail One'* began his low-level, high-speed run. The birds scattered en-mass and rose above the helo like a dark cloud.

"Holy Moley!" 'Louie' screamed to the helo's door-gunner, trying to be heard above the roar of the aircraft.

"That looked like a 'casting call' for the next Hitchcock 'The Birds' movie!"

"You're damn sure right about that, 'Swabby'. I ain't never seen that many birds in one place in all my days!" yelled the Marine Corporal.

Louie busied himself with trying to get his air-to-air and Marine close-ups before his chopper landed, and things got complicated.

As planned, with the pad cleared, *'Yellow Tails Three and Four'* sat down and disgorged their cargoes. So far the plan had worked, but, as the last Marine and ARVN reached the tree-line, the earth began exploding all around. The VC were awake and laying down a devastating field of fire onto the troops.

Mortars, grenades and automatic weapons were chewing up the trees and brush where Louie and the Chief were desperately grinding out their photos.

"Sailor, keep your head down and your eyes peeled," the First Sergeant beside Louie warned him. "These little bastards are like monkeys. Their snipers have a nasty habit of climbing up into the tree-tops, waiting 'til you're almost under them, then picking you off! Keep your eyes moving and watch for any rustling leaves—in the trees <u>or on the ground</u>!"

"LOOK OUT, SARGE !" Louie yelled, as he quickly rolled over, bringing his AR-15 around and unloading four or five rounds into a stand of palms. As the echoes faded, a VC stumbled out from behind the tree on their right and fell dead in the grass.

"Buddy, that was some shooting! Where'd you learn to 'snap shoot' like that?" the Sergeant asked.

"Sarg, as a kid, I used to hunt the bayou for all kinds of varmints—'possoms, 'coons, and such—I could take the head off a cottonmouth at 10 paces, and that ain't no s—t !"

"You get an 'attaboy' from me, Partner," the sergeant chuckled, "That's keeping on your toes. Any closer and we'd have been in grenade throwing range.

"Navy, you stick close to me," the sergeant whispered. *"I like the way you operate !"*

All Louie could think about at the moment was—"I missed getting it on film !"

The firing grew more intense. Rifle and machine gun bullets were chopping up the brush all around. A mortar exploded about twenty five yards from Louie, killing a young baby-faced Marine private. Small bits of shrapnel, twigs and dirt sprinkled down on Louie's helmet, but he remained unscathed.

Louie continued to film and fire, exposing himself for very brief seconds, to not give a sniper time to 'zero-in' on him.

In another part of the forest, Chief Gilmore, along with his combined-Marine/ARVN force, was pinned down by a nest of VC, and were unable to break out.

The firing went on for hours, with no let-up.

The Marine Major, in command of the force, took two sniper bullets to his right shoulder, which put him out of the action and earned him a trip to a MedEvac Hospital and probably a 'Get-Home-Free Ticket'.

The young Captain assumed command and ordered his troops to lay down a heavy fire and try to end the standoff.

In the midst of the heavy fire, Chief Gilmore loaded a full clip in his AR-15 and charged around the left flank, firing on full automatic, swinging the gun from side-to-side, cutting down the brush and trees where the VC were hiding. The Marine Captain later said it was "like he was mowing a wheat field."

What VC were still able to, broke and ran in the face of this red-faced mad-man. At a later count there were eight VC dead or wounded.

The Captain wanted to put the Chief in for a medal but Gilmore strongly objected, saying—

"Cap, I was just finishing what I've been waiting twenty years to do ! I'm finally right with my Korean War Buddies. Thanks, but, no thanks !"

Soon after, the VC disengaged and began to drift off into their jungle hideouts.

The UH1-B helos were called back in and began picking up the wounded and dead, following up with a full retrieval of the 'walking-wounded' and the balance of the force, and returning them to the Pleiku Air Base they had left only thee days before.

A hot shower and a good meal brought Louie and Chief Gilmore back to the 'real world'.

The shock and stress of the experience was still too vivid in their memories to discuss what they had gone through, so they kept the conversation light and jocular, for now. They'd have ample time to recall these days when they wrote up their reports, back in Saigon.

Sleep was illusive so their idle chatter continued on into the wee hours. Exhaustion eventually caught up with them, however, and they finally fell into stupefying coma-like sleep. It was ten hours later that they came to life, refreshed and ready for the trip back to their 'Villa'.

Arriving at the CCG Tan Son Nhut office, the two were greeted with 'beers and cheers' by the rest of team ALPHA-TWO.

"I hear you two got your 'baptism' on this go-'round," Lt. Duncan remarked, "Between Louie's sharp-shooting and Gilmore's 'charge up San Juan Hill', you made quite an impression on those Marines."

"How'd you hear about that, already?" Chief Gilmore inquired.

"Hell, Chief, when the jury-rigged phone lines are acting up we use radios, didn't, you know? We were checking on you as soon as we got word the operation was over," the Lt. chuckled. "Sure glad you both got back here in one piece. Though, Louie, did you get wounded? You've got some blood on your shoulder."

"No Sir. Mr. Duncan, I guess I picked that up from that poor private who got snuffed in the mortar blast. I need to get all my rags to the laundry, pronto, I still smell like something out of the 'Black Lagoon'."

"OK, Guys, Get unpacked and set down with 'Teach' and get all your data sheets typed. He'll make a faster and neater job of it than you apes could. I want your film on today's currier flight to DC. Then you can tell him the details of your experience 'under fire' for the Action Report.

"After that, 'field strip' and clean your photo gear and your weapons. It's Friday so you two can enjoy two days of well-earned 'stand-down' time.

"Seth, you, Baldy and Roger will be saddling up first thing Sunday morning for your chance for 'Glory'," Lt. Duncan warned them.

"The only 'danger' you'll face is a few snakes and 'jungle rot'. You're to catch a flight to Clark Air Force Base in the Philippines.

"CINCPAC (Commander in Chief of the Pacific) has established a 'Jungle Survival School' about midway between Clark and Subic Bay. It's staffed by a half-dozen 'Negritos' (Filipino pigmies). They're a tough little bunch who terrorized the Japanese occupation forces for their entire stay in the island country," Mr. Duncan said, "The head 'honcho' is called 'Sarge', a title he earned in the resistance forces. These guys lived off the jungle and know every trick of getting 'by' on what nature provides.

"Your job will be to come up with an 'in-depth' story about the school. Sound, narration, and lots of close-ups, two-shots and establishing shots.—just like they taught you in USC and mopic school. A real 'production'. It's a challenge, but I know you can do it. RIGHT GUYS ?"

"You betchum, Chief," Baldy agreed. "A regular Cecil B. DeMille saga !"

Seth, and his group fell to assembling the gear they would need for their 'production'—portable battery-powered lights, sound recorders, plenty of film and, of course, a sturdy, light-weight tripod, two Arriflex™ cameras and two Nikons™ (two each in case of a break down.).

"Man, with all this gear to 'hump' around, we'll all need hernia-braces by the time we finish this job," Roger complained.

"Don't start bitchin' yet, Roger," Seth answered, "We'll be out in the 'boonies' the whole time and what we need, <u>WE CARRY</u>! Maybe we can pick up a couple 'pack horses' (junior Photo-Mates) from the lab in Subic., to give us a hand."

"I sure hope so, podner," Baldy added.

Chief Gilmore and Louie completed their Data Sheets and Action Report, along with 'Teach's' help, and were ready to 'knock off'—but first—they made a visit to the CCG 'Villa' where they changed out of their smelly fatigues and, not satisfied with the shower they had in Pleiku, showered again, for 20 to 30 minutes with <u>strong deodorant</u> soap. Their scroungy clothes were dropped off at the Chinese cleaners and life was finally back to normal,—which meant—off to the Club for a round of 'COOL ONES' (on Lt. Duncan ! of course.).

It was a noisy bunch in the Club, that Friday night, but who could blame "Those Crazy Camera Guys" of CCG for celebrating? Every one wanted to buy the Chief and Louie a beer which naturally led to two very inebriated sailors before their buddies carried them off to the 'Villa' and poured them into their bunks.

It was noon before either of them eased out of bed with queasy stomachs and splitting skulls.

The ordeal didn't slow up the two for long, though. They were back to their normal good natures before sundown.

"You can't keep a good 'swabby' down," bragged Louie.

THREE

Sunday dawned, and Seth and his team headed for the flight-line before the sun had dimmed the street lights. Their flight was slated for a 0700 lift-off and they were determined not to be late for their first assignment.

The plane that was to carry them to the Philippines, was already turning up when they arrived. They quickly shuttled their gear from the van to the aircraft and found seats along the wall. This flight was not configured for passengers—they were transporting wounded troops to Tripler Army Hospital in Hawaii for further treatment and rehabilitation.

The stop-over at Clark Field was to be brief. They would refuel and pick up a few more victims of the Vietnam slaughter-house, then proceed to Hawaii.

"You Navy guys won't have much time to unload your stuff, so make it quick," the Cargo Master, an Air Force Sergeant, yelled to them, over the roar of the jets, "We'll be back in the air in 15 minutes, or, as soon as we refuel, which ever comes first!"

With the assistance of a couple of the ground-crew members, Seth, Baldy and Roger, had everything piled on a flat-bed cart and, piling atop, they were swiftly carried off the flight-line to the terminal.

"Will the Navy Photo team please meet your contact at the Navy Liaison desk." The terminal public-address system blared.

"OK, guys, that's us. Let's find this here 'liaison desk'," Seth said, "Roger, you stay with the gear and don't take your eye off it, while Baldy and I go scouting. Be back in a skosh (US sailors' corruption for the Japanese word for short)."

"Aye, Aye, Skipper."

Seth and Baldy were back in moments, accompanied by a Navy Lieutenant in khaki., who Seth introduced as "Lt. Richard Harper, Community Affairs Officer for Subic Bay Naval Station."

"We're going to put you men up in Guest Housing here for the night and we'll all get a fresh start, bright and early, in the morning," announced the Lt.

"That's great. I think I and my guys can stand a bit of shut-eye after that long, hemorrhoid aggravating flight," Seth agreed.

A gigantic meal at the NCO club, and a sound night's sleep, had the team ready to get on the job at sun-up.

"I'll be your liaison between the Filipino head-instructor, known as 'Sarge'. Anything you require to do your job, I'm the guy to supply it. 'Sarge' is going to meet us at the camp and give you the 'lay' of the land," Lt. Harper told the three. "I've heard that, in 'Nam they say 'CCG doesn't stand for 'Combat Camera Group' but 'CRAZY CAMERA GUYS'. Well, CinCPac expects a serious documentary from you guys so refrain from any shenanigans."

"Lieutenant, don't worry. We take our work <u>very</u> serious. We reserve our jokes and banter to our personal, off the job, interactions." Seth reassured the officer, "It's our way of staying SANE in this INSANE 'war'."

"Good!" the Lt. replied. "Now, I have ¾ ton vehicle waiting for us, so load up and we'll head into the jungle."

"HOOKA-HAI !" Roger shouted, "I had a 'Lakota Sioux' Indian in my 'boot camp' company, and he said that means—'Let's get out 'a here' !"

"Well Roger, in 'Nam we say 'di-di mau', but, however you want to say it, 'let's move it' !" Seth returned.

The trip to the camp was fine—until they left the main road and started up an-unpaved, poor excuse for a road—. The four-wheel-drive vehicle struggled and strained to stay on solid ground and, the Navy driver fought every inch of the way, trying to maneuver over all the stones and roots.

After about an hour of this punishment, the driver pulled into a clearing and stopped, with a final jolt, in front of a 'hard-back' tent. Standing around were five small, dark-skinned men, none of whom stood over 4 ½ feet tall. These were the Negrito Pigmy's, here to impart their jungle-survival savvy to the Navy and Marine students due to arrive tomorrow.

Introductions were made all around and then Lt. Harper suggested he and the team meet with 'Sarge' to plan a shooting schedule for rest of the week.

"I'm thinking, 'Sarge' can give you guys an overview of how the school operates," the Lt. says, "Then you experts can decide on what will best tell the tale."

"Good idea, Lt.," added Seth, "I brought my portable 'Remington'™, so let's bat around a few ideas while I type up the notes."

This kept the photojournalists busy working their brain cells, separating the 'grain from the chaff'.

Three hours of intense concentration, produced a working plan, which the Lt. and the entire assemblage agreed, should present CinCPac with the documentation of the Jungle Survival School which CinCPac would approve.

"One thing I think we should, emphasize in the story," Seth commented, "is this school teaches these men how to live 'off-the-land'. It's unlike the 'SEAR' school back in Borrego Springs, which concentrated on how to resist and escape, if captured. Here the 'Negrito' instructors will show how to **AVOID** getting captured and how to survive to fight another day."

"That I'll vote for," commented Baldy, "I sure don't care to think about finishing my career sitting in one of those VC 'Monkey Cages' !"

"OK, guys, the rest of the day I want you assembling the gear you'll need for the scenes we'll be shooting tomorrow," Seth ordered, "The students will be here in the morning. Lt. Harper says there'll be 3 Marine pilots, 2 Navy pilots, an enlisted River Boat skipper, and an Army helo jockey. These are the typical men who might find themselves stranded in the jungles of 'Nam.

"The 'Sarge' wants his instructors assigned one to every two students. We'll alternate coverage on each team so as to tie the whole 'shebang' together. I think we CCG mugs should stay together and work in unison—still, mopic and sound/narration.

"Remember, this is a documentary. We need a wide-range of close-ups, two-shots and establishing (over-all) scenes. We're telling a story and we have to have good continuity throughout."

The cameramen started feverishly sorting through their many cases of equipment and, amid their chatter and light-hearted banter, soon had their back-packs loaded with their 'tools of the trade'.

"Hey, Seth!" said Roger, "We're all set and 'ready-for-teddy'—whoever 'TEDDY' is."

"OK, Men, let's take a break. Play it COOL, eat your last **civilized** meal you'll have for the next week, and get a good night's sleep," the Lt. advised, "Tomorrow we 'go native' and learn to eat grubs, snails and other such delicacies."

"Snails I've had in the bayou, in garlic and butter, but that other crap, forget it!" Baldy piped up, "If I have eat them, I'll puke!"

"You'd be surprised what you can get down, if you get hungry enough," Lt. Harper said.

The shooting went off without a 'hitch' until the third day. Baldy had been filming one of the instructors demonstrating how to get pure-clear water out of a bamboo stalk by chopping into a section with his machete and catching the water that came out and dribbled into his canteen.

Well, Baldy decided he was going to try it—BIG mistake—he forgot to notice that the stalk had to be gripped above the adjoining knuckle. Holding the bamboo in the same section he was chopping into, the stalk suddenly split and snapped shut on the heel of Baldys' hand, opening up a one-inch flap of hide.

Baldys' screams echoed throughout the jungle for miles around. The negrito immediately cut off a piece of a milkweed-like plant and squeezed the flowing sap under and on the hanging skin.

"That fix it," he assured the sobbing sailor, slapping on a strip of tape. "This good medicine. Be fine tomorrow."

The next day, sure enough, the wound was closed up and appeared to be healing as though it had happened a week ago !

"Now you guys have had a lesson in jungle-lore," Lt Harper told the photographers and students. "Study that plant and remember what to look for. It might save your life sometime."

This was just one of many jungle-survival tricks the men were shown during the week's say in the Philippine jungle.

On the final day of their filming the photo team returned to camp and Seth swiftly began typing up the data sheets. Meanwhile the other two packaged up the film and sound tapes for shipment back to CinCPac on the first courier flight out of Clark Air Force Base.

"We'll get your men back to Clark tonight so your stuff can catch the next flight." said Harper. "You can bunk-down in the 'Guest House' again, tonight, and get a flight back to Vietnam sometime tomorrow."

"I'd really rather be going along with our film, if it's all the same to you, Lt.," came from Baldy.

"DREAM ON my hairy friend." was Seth's reply, "but I would like to say, I think we did a bang-up job and CinCPac and Lt. Duncan should be pleased with the results of this past week's efforts. Bravo Zulu, guys."

Chief Gilmore and the rest of team ALPHA-TWO hadn't been 'sitting on their tails' while their shipmates were busy in the Philippines.

Action in 'Nam hadn't ceased during the ensuing week—if anything, it had 'heated up' considerably.

Chief Gilmore and 'Louie' deployed with a couple Marine patrols and later, were sent along on 'Operation River Sweep' on the Mekong Delta.

In this, the VC had ambushed two US Riverine RPBs (River Patrol Boats) near Kien Long and two 'shufly' helo rescue ships were being dispatched to retrieve the two crews.

Chief Gilmore and Louie' boarded, one to each craft,. and began filming the helo crews and the terrain flashing by below. The rescue zone was about a 45 minute speed-run and the door gunner stood ready to shower the VC with his 'Ma Deuce' (M-2) machine gun.

As they neared the site, the boat skipper popped a yellow smoke to show their location. The VC were scattered about the banks of the small river.

"Bluebird Two, this is Bluebird leader. Let's make a couple passes and see if we can't 'snuff' a few of those gooks, before we begin our attempt for extraction"

"*Roger, Bluebird Leader. A few grenades and our M-2s ought to set 'em back on their heels. Maybe give us a few minutes unhampered approach to our guys!*"

Both the Chief and Louie were hanging out the side doors, restrained by only a three-foot gunner's belt, burning film of the action, their only thoughts were, '*Get the pictures first, worry about the risk later*'.

After both helos had completed two passes with grenades and guns raining death and destruction on the VC ambushers, *Bluebird Leader* made the first move to pick up the crew of the disabled boat. One minute over target and he had the crew dangling on the rope ladder and moved out to allow *Bluebird Two* clearance to make his run. By this time the VC were regrouping and beginning to fire at *Bluebird Two*.

"*Bluebird Leader, this is Bluebird Two, I'm taking fire,. Can you assist?*"

"*It'll take a 'skosh' getting the last of our young 'uns aboard. Be right there!*"

In an instant *Bluebird Leader* had retrieved the rescued first boat crew and rushed to aid *Bluebird Two*.

"*Here we come to save the day!*" Bluebird Leader radioed.

"*OK, 'Mighty Mouse'. We can sure use your help. I'm just picking up the last of my marbles. Let's 'boogie' out of this hornets nest, PRONTO!*"

"*Bluebird Two, this is Bluebird Leader, I'm going to make one more high-speed 'go-around'. I still have some ammo left I'd like to leave it as a parting gift with those 'slope-heads'!*"

"*Roger, Bluebird Leader. I'll be right on your 'six'!*"

With their ammo expended, the rescuers and the rescued '*di-di mau-ed*' for home.

On the ground, after quick hugs all around from the RPB crews, the helo crews inspected their aircraft.

"I count four holes in my bird," *Bluebird Two* pilot, Warrant Officer Robert Bowen said. "Man that was 'hairy'. Thanks to you and your crew, Skipper, we survived to fly another mission."

"Well, we didn't come away unscathed, either." *Bluebird Leader*, Warrant Officer Clyde Donavan replied. "There's two holes just aft of my seat. Six inches more toward the nose and I'd 'a had my ass burned. Can't get much luckier than that, I'd say."

The Chief and Louie both said a prayer of 'THANKS', as they picked up their camera gear and hopped on their waiting van.

"Home, James !" Chief Gilmore instructed Teach, who was at the wheel. "I can use a good shower and clean scivvies. After which I'm buying the first round at the NCO Club!"

"And I'm springing' for the second. Then, it's every men for himself!" Louie added.

Seth and his crew arrived almost simultaneously, and flagged down Teach at the terminal and all returned to the 'Villa' en masse

The Club was a riotous place that night—what with CCG and the Marine flyboys all celebrating at the same time. Several cases of beer washed away the day's excitement in no time and all staggered home in the wee hours.

The sun was barely over the horizon when Chief Gilmore roused the sleeping beauties by banging on a trash can.

"Alright you 'Goof-offs', rise and shine. Drop your c—ks and grab your socks, IT'S REVEILLE ! Not just a few, THE WHOLE DAMN CREW, IT'S REVEILLE !!"

"Have a heart, Chief," Baldy complained, "We all had a rough night."

"Too bad, Baldy," the chief replied, "So did I, but we have work to do first, then we can do our 'recuperating'.

"*Priority number one*, Louie. You and I have to get the film from our escapade yesterday, on the plane to DC. ***Priority*** *number two*, everybody needs to field-day your cameras and weapons to be ready for the next 'waltz' we get invited to. And don't forget you laundry !"

"Yeah," piped up Louie, "***Cleanliness is next to Godliness,*** I hear, and I could use a whole lot of both!"

The chores finally completed, the Chief informed them that they could 'stand down' until Monday—baring any emergencies.

"A word of advice, Guys," Lt. Duncan added, "Stay away from those girls at 'Mama Wu's'. I find out you've been messing with one, it's an automatic forfeiture of a weeks pay. The second time, it'll be a month's pay. Any questions?"

"Yeah, Mr. Duncan," 'Louis' asked, "How much is a season's pass?"

Saturday afternoon, Roger returned to the 'Villa' dirty and bruised.

"'What the hell happened to you?" Lt Duncan asked on seeing his battered condition.

"I turned my ankle and bruised my shoulder dodging a cyclo (motorcycle/rickshaw hybrid)."

"Roger, you gotta' quit chasing them things. Just stand on the curb and another one will come along."

"Lt., you don't understand, I <u>was</u> standing on the curb. <u>That's</u> when he **hit** <u>me</u>. The sombitch didn't even stop !"

"Well, Son, get yourself patched up and into a clean set of fatigues. I'm sure that's not going to put a permanent crimp in your weekend."

"Damn, Lt., I think it's safer out in the 'boonies' than on the streets of Saigon. These drivers are plumb loco !"

"You damn sure got that right, Roger," Seth agreed, "I've had my britches singed a few times, myself, trying to dodge those kamikaze little bastards.!"

"Well, Fellows," the Lt. added, "Just avoid playing 'matador' and be sure you 'ZIG' when they 'ZAG'. That way, we might **possibly** survive in this here 'demolition derby'."

During the stand-down, Roger spent his free time in the Saigon USO—HE WAS IN LOVE !

Learning of Roger's affliction drew Lieutenant Duncan's extreme wrath.

"You heard my message 'LOUD and CLEAR ! when I warned you Romeos about messing with these Vietnamese girls !" the Lt. stormed, "I should pull your stripes for disobeying my orders, you numb skull !"

"But, Lt.," Roger tried to explain, "Xuan's not one of these Le Loi Street hookers. She's one of the managers at the USO. Yes, she was born over here. Her father was an American, working here as an aide to the American Consular General. He met Anne's (Vietnamese name 'Xuan') mother in the Embassy, where she was also employed. They got married in the Embassy and later Xuan was born.

"Xuan's mother, a mix of Chinese and Vietnamese, died during the French-Indo-Chinese War and Xuan's father decided it was too dangerous to try to raise his eight-year-old daughter over here, so he took her back to the States. She's US-educated and a hell of a lot smarter the I am. She has a degree in Socio-economics from The University of Oregon.

"When this fracas started up and the USO started establishing Canteens over here, they recruited Anne to return to help out. Her fluency in French, Chinese, Vietnamese and English made her a valuable asset

"We're waiting 'til my tour is up and we can go back to Michigan and be married with my family and her father present.—NO, we haven't been having sex !—We both have religious and cultural beliefs against that—unlike Baldy and a lot of other men over here ! Anne's an American citizen so getting hitched in the US, we'll have no 'Red-Tape' to have to fight through."

"Roger, I have to apologize for assuming the worst." Lt. Duncan responded, "It sounds like you two are really serious and have thought this out pretty well. I'd like to meet your 'dream-girl' one of these days."

"You'd like her Lt. She's the prettiest thing I ever saw. Porcelain complexion, almond-shaped eyes and skin the color of over-creamed coffee."

"WOW," Louie marveled, "I wish I'd met her first !"

"She's TOO MUCH for the likes of you, Louie. You wouldn't make it out of the batter's box."

The gang gathered 'round and shook Roger's hand and congratulated him. There was no off-colored remarks or teasing about this—everyone realized Roger was really serious.

The mood had grown somber and Louie tried to lighten things up by dragging out his clarinet and making a vain attempt at playing the 'wedding march'—which brought on boo's and 'cat-calls' until he gave up.

FOUR

The two-day 'stand-down' flew by and was over before the men hardly had enough time to 're-charge' their bodily and equipment batteries.

"Vacation's over, Gang," Lt. Duncan announced, returning from his morning conference with the CinCPac and Seventh Fleet Detachment media reps. "There's some things going on, in the next couple days, that we're going to have to cover. So gather 'round and we can map out our assignments."

"Lt.," Seth spoke up. "I hope there's going to be some action. Me 'n Baldy and Roger had it pretty tame last week while the Chief and Louie were mixin' it up. We aren't 'glory-hounds', but we want to do our share and take our chances, like the rest of the team."

"Don't worry, Seth, with what's in the pot, you'll all get to see plenty of 'action'." the Lt. reassured him.

"As usual, <u>ALL</u> 'Operations' we're assigned to cover are EXTEMELY HUSH-HUSH, so 'zip your lips'. First off, we'll be going in with a major force dubbed 'Operation Piranha' to drive the VC out of the Batangan Peninsula, near a town called Quang Ngai, about one hundred 'clicks' southeast of Da Nang. The Marines will be hitting them from the beach, so plan on getting your feet wet. Take along plenty of those plastic 'C' ration bags to keep your gear dry," the Lieutenant further advised.

"There'll be a strong resistance force in the area, and heavy casualties are expected—just don't you guys be one of them !—in spite of your shenanigans I still love you. Chief Gilmore and I will sit down this morning and decide who goes where. The rest of you, start packing. Take only what you can't do without—you need to travel light—plenty of film, your cameras and a couple changes of socks and scivvies, and, of course, your weapons!

"Does that sound like enough 'excitement' for you, Seth?"

"Just point the way, Sir, I'm READY!" was his quick reply.

The team had 24 hours before they were given the order to board helos and proceed to an LST (Landing Ship Transport) off Da Nang on 'Yankee Station' (South China Sea).

Once aboard, the five men were assigned to separate Marine Companies with whom they would make their landings. Each Company was lead by a Marine Captain or higher from whom the photographers would be taking directions.

"We don't want any unnecessary casualties." the Marine CO, warned, "The 'Tin Cans' (Destroyers) off shore will be laying down heavy bombardment so we have to be extra cautious not to over-run their 'kill zone'.

"We shove-off at 0430, so get some sleep, if you can, and be ready to give 'Charley' HELL!"

The seas were smooth as silk at 0430 and the landing craft, taking the men to the beach, made a speed run all the way to the high-tide line before the VC and NVA (North Vietnam Regular Army) caught on to what was happening. All the troops were well into the tree-line before meeting any resistance. From there on it was a tree-to-tree fight, lasting five-to-six hours with the enemy taking heavy casualties. The Marines faired some better, but even <u>one loss</u> was one too many.

By sundown, the VC and NVA had had enough and slithered off into the dense jungle.

Seth and Roger had encountered a hot-spot and had to fire their weapons, all the while trying to film the action. Roger's AK-47 got so hot he had to lay-low until it was cool enough for him to resume his frantic firing. Seth was doing a little better. He had taken cover behind a fallen palm log, and was alternately filming and shooting.

The only 'injury' they received was, Roger's AK-47 had given him a <u>very</u> black-and-blue shoulder.

"Roger, If you'd used both hands, you'd have accomplished more," Seth remarked.

"What the Hell, man. D'ya think I'm ambidextrous, or something'?"

"I don't give a hoot what religion you are. Just giving you a little advise,"

"Huh! A 'little advice' from you is more than I need right now!"

The other two team members, Seth and Baldy, came out of the fracas unscathed, but shaken up.

"I hope Seth got his wish for 'action'." said the Chief, "If he didn't, he should have been with my company! Man the bullets were whizzing around us like a tipped-over hornets' nest. If those 'Jar-heads' hadn't been so effective, we'd probably all be face-down in the jungle mud!"

"It wasn't a bed-of-roses where I was, either, Chief," Baldy added, "I saw three good Marines get cut down ten minutes after we hit the beach. Those damn 'fish-eaters' were dug in like gophers in a California golf course. You pick one off and another pops up and tries to burn ya'. I think I got some good footage, but it's hard to tell, what with a camera in one hand and a rifle in the other. I'm just thankful I'm small enough to hunker down in the brush., but, they were chewin' up the bushes all around me. I had to stick my Arriflex up for a couple seconds, run off a few feet of film, duck down and then try to pick off the 'gooks' with my AK-47 that were trying to 'snuff' me."

"Well, we made it out of that sh—t, this time." Gilmore agreed, "I guess my old 'Irish Luck' is still holding. I thought I'd used it all up in Korea."

"You Mutts got off easy," Louie piped up, "My Marines and I ran into a bunch of NVA with 'tak san' (many) grenades and they proceeded to pepper our butts with them. Thank God, none of them had ever played Little League. They were missing us by a mile—most of the time—all except for one who fancied himself the VC 'Bob Feller'. He lobbed one about ten feet from me and my Sergeant. The Sarge took shrapnel in his thigh and I got 1/2 inch chunk in my 'gluteus maximas'—that's 'BUTT'—to you illiterates," remarked Louie.

"Listen to our little Cajun Swamp Rat, spouting Latin would you," was Seth's come-back.

"Hey. We got edu macation in Louisiana, too !" was Louies' laughing reply.

"Sh—t, Louie, now you'll be the first on our team to get a Purple Heart. Dumb Luck!" Baldy complained.

'Like HELL I'll take a PH. Can you just imagine, when I go back to New Orleans, how I'd ever explain **where** I was wounded to get that medal? I'd be the laughing stock of the Bayou. **NEBBA HAPP'N CAP'N ! !**

"The Sarge dug out the chunk of metal, sprinkled on some Sulpha and slapped a 'band aid' on it and I'm fine. I'll hang onto the shrapnel, though, as a reminder to keep my butt down, like Chief Gilmore tried to teach me !"

The team was trucked back to Da Nang for transport to Saigon. But, before they could hop a flight, Lt. Duncan showed up.

"Guys, we're not going back to Saigon just yet. ComNavForV (Commander Naval Forces Vietnam) has asked that we do an 'update' on the hospital here. It's finished and up and running now. They're doing a 'numba one' job of patching up the wounded from I Corps, and the 'Brass' want to play it up for the folks back in 'The World'."

"Sounds good to me," Seth answered, "I've been hearing they set a might scrumptious table, and we 'uns could all go for some good, hot chow. 'C-rats' just don't suit my palate."

"**AMEN** to that !" the whole team replied.

"So, all right then. Hop back on that truck and we'll 'commandeer' it to haul us over to the hospital.," Mr. Duncan ordered.

True to the rumors, the hospital put on a feed unequaled in Vietnam as well as most other parts of the Far East.

The staff of the hospital 'rolled out' the welcome mat for the photo team, and, after stuffing themselves and a good night's sleep, Gilmore turned loose the crew to film 'everything in sight'.

They worked feverishly for two days and came away with what the CO, in his comments to the departing guys, said:

"I'd say you men did yourselves, and the hospital mighty proud— Bravo Zulu !—The Navy Bureau of Medicine will be able to put your film to good use. It'll be a tremendous boost to their PR"

Their first morning back in SAIGON, the men were greeted by Lt. Duncan, following his morning briefing by 7ᵗʰ Fleet Detachment Operations.

"Gentlemen, I have GOOD news and BAD news. Which would you like to hear first?"

"Sir, give us the bad news first. I always like my dessert last," Baldy replied.

"OK. The bad news is my tour is up in three weeks and my relief will be here next week. No word, yet, who it'll be. The GOOD news is, I'll make it back to 'The World' in time for Christmas !"

"Lt. that's good news for you but BAD news for us," Chief Gilmore moaned.

"Right, I sure hope it ain't 'Hard Nose' Hennesey," Louie commented. "He'd fit in this group like a dirty sock in a drawer of 'Victoria's Secret™' ' lingerie!"

"Let's play it cool, guys," Lt. Duncan advised the team, "My replacement will be reporting to the Yokosuka Office later this week. Then, he'll arrive in Saigon about the middle of the next week. That'll give us about ten days to get this place ship shape. I want you yard birds to get off on the right foot, no matter who'll be your next OinC."

"**Let us pray !**"was Baldie's retort.

The 'word' was slow in geting to ALPHA-TWO, but, two days later, to their intense satisfaction, they learned the new OinC was Lt. HARVEY CROCKET, a resent graduate of the Navy Motion Picture Directors Class at USC.

"I know this guy," said Seth, "He's a man of our 'cloth', he'll fit in great."

"Seth, if you say he's 'JAKE', he must be the kind of officer we can work for," Chief Gilmore said, "We really need someone who can understand this bunch, if we are to keep on functioning."

"OK, Guys, when he gets here, let's soft-pedal our shenanigans for a while. Give him a chance to adjust to you nutty 'yard birds'," Lt. Duncan ordered, "Right now we need to 'turn-to' and finish getting the Tan Son Nhut office and the 'Villa' 'field-day-ed'. I want him to see we're not all play and no work."

Lt. Crocket's flight from Japan arrived at Tan Son Nhut Airport the next afternoon and he was met by the CCG van with Lt. Duncan at the wheel and Chief Gilmore 'riding shot-gun'.

"Hope you had a smooth flight, Harvey," Mr. Duncan greeted him, "But, I warn you, the most exciting part of the trip is yet to come! I know you're from up-state New York, but, if you've ever had to drive Times Square in rush hour traffic, or the West-Side Highway, you're in for a ride like you've never before experienced. I've been here almost six months and I still drive 'white-knuckled'.

"These Saigon wheel jockeys don't 'drive' their vehicle—they AIM it, and go 'pedal to the metal'. Woe be to anything that doesn't jump out their way !"

"Lieutenant, you've got me scared, already !" Lt. Crocket admitted.

Lt. Harvey Crocket is a long-time Navy Photo Mate. He joined the Navy at seventeen, and, from 'Boot Camp', he was sent to Pensacola, Florida to the Naval School of Photography. He subsequently served assignments on various ships and stations, rising to the rating of Petty Officer First Class. With high evaluation marks, and an exemplary record, he was offered OCS (Officer Candidate School).

Immediately following completion of 'knife-and-fork' training,—now a commissioned Ensign (Limited Duty)—he was given orders to USC to attend a year of Navy Movie Directors schooling.

His career had progressed without incident, up to NOW, abiding by rules and regs.—but now he was in for a new way of life, brought on by MAJOR CHANGES in this, his first taste of command. This situation would tax his ability to adapt !

"We have to make a stop at the office to pick up a couple of our photogs, then it's into the 'Demolition Derby', as we've so aptly named our nightly run from the Office to our 'Villa'." Lt. Duncan informed the new OinC.

At the Office, Baldy had some worrisome news.

"Lt., 7th Fleet Ops just informed us Tu Do street is blocked by a fender-bender and we'll have to detour around it. We've been studying our map, and found a possible alternate route. It's an unimproved road, but the latest word is it's been free of any VC activity for over a week. Though I think we'd best play it safe and carry our 'artillery'."

"OK, I thoroughly agree. Better safe than sorry !" Lt. Duncan replied, "Let's get armed and don't forget extra ammo! Pile in and let's move out !

"Baldy, you have the map so you 'ride shotgun' for me and navigate the route." Duncan directed.

"Harvey, I sure hope this doesn't turn out to be your 'baptism' ! Everyone be on high-alert. If any 'Charlies' do show up, I don't want any casualties this late in my tour," the Lt. said, "Only two-and-a-half more weeks and I'm home safe."

"We'll make damn sure we get you out of our hair without a scratch on the merchandise, Lieutenant," Seth reassured him.

When Baldy called the road 'unimproved' he over-evaluated the shape of this un-surfaced, rutted and pot-hole filled 'water buffalo path'. Fortunately the locals didn't relish traversing this narrow road, either, so they didn't encounter any other traffic.

"If we met so much as a bicycle along here, one of us would wind up on the side of this path with our wheels in that 'binjo' ditch (open sewage run-off ditch)," Lt. Duncan groaned.

To make a bad situation worse, at one of the most isolated sections,—a thousand yards from the nearest ramshackle 'hooch' where children swam and splashed in the polluted water,—the van sputtered and quit.

"NOW WHAT?" Baldy exclaimed.

"It appears, gentlemen as though we've run out of petrol !" Seth informed the weary travelers, "Our little Cajun numb-scull drove the van back from the Office last night just before curfew. My last instruction to him was, before leaving Tan Son Nhut, to gas it up!!"

"Well, Seth," Baldy piped up, "I might suggest—LOUIE was the only thing that was 'GASSED UP' last night !"

"Yeah. I heard him drive the van through the gate an instant before curfew." added Roger, "I was surprised he didn't take out the side of the 'Villa', but he got it parked and shut it down OK. But, when he got a couple feet from his sack, he fell across it and that's the same position he was in this morning when I got up."

"Right now, we need a couple volunteers to hike down to that shack before dark and see if they have some gas we can borrow.—Don't all speak at once !" Chief Gilmore asked.

"Chief, I'll go," Roger spoke up, "Anne's been teaching me some Vietnamese and French. I think I can stumble through the language problem better than any of these other numb-skulls."

"Good thinking, Sailor. Who's going with him?"

"I'll go," Baldy answered.

"Be alert, Guys," Lt. Duncan told them, "You don't know what kind of reception you might run into."

The two men took off and very shortly came trudging back followed by a Vietnamese boy leading a huge water buffalo.

"Lieutenant, they didn't have any gas, but 'Bac', here says he'll give us a tow down the road about a click (kilometer) to a gas station. I gave them some Snickers™ and they're happy as pigs in sh—t. I offered them some piasters, but they preferred the gee-dunks to money."

"'Never look a gift horse—or maybe that should be a water buffalo—in the mouth', I always say." chuckled Lt. Crocket.

"I told you he was our kinda' guy, didn't I?" Seth bragged. "And I have some very appropriate words for Louie when I see him. ! !"

"I'm thinking that loaning him to the Army Hospital for a couple days of 'house-cleaning' and bed-pan dumping might make him think, next time," Lt. Duncan replied

"I LIKE IT ! !" they all shouted in unison.

FIVE

When the team arrived back at the 'Villa', following their roadside adventure, Louie was greeted with snarls and unspeakable comments—unspeakable by all but these CCG angry members.

"When you guys have finished letting off your steam," remarked Lt. Duncan, "I want the pleasure of informing Louie what his punishment is for not following orders."

Louie's cries of anguish, on hearing what he'd be doing the next two days, could be heard all the way back to Tan Son Nhut.

"I'm sorry, Guys. I had a bit too much of old 'barley-corn' and it just slipped my mind !"

"**A BIT TOO MUCH ! !** he calls it. He came home snockered out of his gourd !" Roger exclaimed.

"In addition to the Hospital duties, I also order you to lay off' **'the old barley corn'**, OR BEER ! For two weeks !" Lt. Duncan further instructed Louie.

'Jeeze, Lt., Have a heart," 'Louie pleaded.

"I think, next time you down a cool one, you'll realize, what you do, effects every guy in this unit, and you'll slow down. We're a team as long as we're responsible to everyone else, <u>UNDERSTOOD.</u>?"

"Aye, Aye, Sir. Understood."

"And, at the risk of 'preaching'—which I dislike as much as y'all do—I want all of you to think about what I just said. **WE'RE A TEAM !**"

"Gather 'round, men," Lt. Duncan ordered. "Last night I had dinner at the 'O' Club and sat at the table with the CO of the SeaBee battalions in country. I asked him what the story was on our 'rolling blackouts' we have to endure every three or four nights. He said to blame that on the VC up in the 'Highlands'. They have a bad habit of trying to knock out our power plant near DaLat, and five nights ago, did massive damage to a couple of the big generators there. That plant supplies more than half the electricity for Saigon and the suburbs.

"The SeaBees are laboring 24/7 to get it back to full capacity. I asked permission to send our team up there to document the repair operations. He gave us a hearty 'go ahead'. I want the whole team to 'di-di' up there tomorrow.and give saturation coverage of their efforts.

'SENIOR Chief Brady and his ALPHA-ONE team were there three or four months ago and brought back some excellent footage of these hard working men. While there, they came under siege by a dozen, or so, 'sappers' trying to lay satchel-charges in the plant. These tough SeaBees, with a little help from Brady's team managed to kill five of them and drive the rest off.

"This time, I want you to be on you toes—get the pictures but be ready to help wherever you're needed—whether it's with your weapons of with pick and shovels.

"A Marine Lt. Col., at our table, said he was also going to send a couple of squads of heavily armed Marines up there to provide security for the SeaBees so they could do their repairs without having to fight off 'Charlie' every day."

"That'll maybe help us concentrate on gettin' our pix, too," Chief Gilmore added.

"Yeah," piped up Baldy, "It ain't no fun trying to handle a camera while we're fighting off a bunch of hornets."

"You CCG guys will be flying out in 48 hours on one of the CIAs aircraft. The 'airstrip' up there in De Lat is too short to handle anything bigger than a C47, and even that's a 'controlled crash' situation—come in high and drop down steeply, touch the wheels, and **put on the brakes**!—According to what Senior Chief Brady told me about his trip last spring," Lt. Duncan told the men.

"Hey, I heard about that 'trip'," Teach replied, "What I heard, they had a pilot they got to calling 'Smilin' Jack'. He had a mustache, wore the crumpled pilot's cap, the leather jacket and the same kind of colored flight glasses—the whole 'maggillla'. He even flew like he was a fighter-pilot.

"When they got to Da Lat, there was heavy cloud cover and the co-pilot suggested turnin' around and coming back later in the day, but, good ol' 'Smilin' Jack' thought he saw an opening in the clouds and took a sharp side-slipping turn and sliced through the clouds, breaking out at roof-top level over the town.

"Lil' Ceasar claimed he looked out his window and saw the church steeple whiz by at eye-level," Teach concluded.

"Man, I sure hope 'Smilin' Jack' ain't still around. I'm runnin' out of clean scivvies," Roger complained.

Their luck was holding, though. The pilot they drew looked nothing like 'Smilin' Jack'. He was older and looked like he'd been 'down the road' a few times. Probably about ready to retire So, their flight went smooth and quiet—enough for some of them to catch a few 'z-z-z's.

The Marines, because of the weaponry they were bringing, were coming in a two-truck convoy and would arrive a day or two later, depending on road conditions and providing 'Charlie' didn't slow them up.

Among the artillery they were bringing to the 'party' was—two 80mm mortars, two WW II 105mm howitzers, three 'Ma-Deuces' (M-2 .50 caliber) machine-guns, a couple of M-79 Grenade launchers—as well as their usual AR-15s and side-arms. These guys were prepared to 'do battle' with any VC foolish enough to challenge them!

The photo team was met by a CB with a six-by truck, which the men quickly loaded up with their gear.

"I'm BU 2 (builder second class) Johnny Jacobs. You guys can hold off on your intros until we get to camp, so you won't have to go over it all again when you meet our CO and the Master Chief," said the CB, "The chow is good and the quarters are about as good as you'll find outside of Saigon. We try not to get **too** military (within reason) and operate much like a civilian construction crew—which most of us were before signing up or were drafted."

It was a winding, bumpy road getting to the camp, but all arrived safe, with only a few bruised posteriors and stiff hands from gripping the wooden seats.

"You can store your camera gear in that shed over there marked '# 6'," instructed Petty Officer Jacobs, "It's secure and we keep it locked, so your gear will be safe.—besides which, we have sentries patrolling the camp 24/7.

"When you finish unloading I'll take you to meet the CO and Master Chief Holliday. They would have been here to welcome you but, they're in the midst of going over the blueprints, figuring tomorrow's repair schedule.

"The damn VC made a hell of a mess when they hit us last week. We just got the replacement parts delivered yesterday, and Lt. Carson, our CO, wants to get 'humpin' early in the morning."

"I can savy that," Chief Gilmore replied, "Me and my team'd like to get to work ASAP, also."

BU 2 Jacobs led the team over to Lt. Carson's quarters and Chief Gilmore made the introductions.

"Chief, we were pleased to have Senior Chief Brady and his crew here last spring. They did a 4.0 job. Our folks back home wrote that they saw some of the film on TV news and the 'home-towners' showed up in several local papers. We're determined to give you all the cooperation we can.

"If there's anything you need, just tell Petty Officer Jacobs and he'll be your liaison with me and the Master Chief. We hope your stay with us will be less exciting than Senior Chief Brady and his bunch experienced."

"Yeah, we heard about the little 'picnic' 'Charlie' threw for them while they were here. Sure glad no one was hurt in that one—and pray we'll leave here with a whole skin, too" Seth commented.

"I second that !" Baldy added.

When 'Reveille' sounded at the crack of dawn, the camp started buzzing with activity. The SeaBees roared up to the refueling trucks and topped off their tanks—and, after a quick breakfast—took off for the power plant to begin their repair chores. Gilmore's men gathered up their gear and piled into a personnel carrier with Petty Officer Jacobs at the wheel.

Jacobs maneuvered the vehicle along the twisting, winding road (?) barely avoiding going over the steep embankment on the left and colliding with the overhanging boulders on the right.

"Hey, Jacobs," Seth yelled, over the racket of the PC as it barreled along, "As we were leaving the camp, I noticed what looked like the foundation of some big building over near the tree-line. What was that?"

"That's what's left of a huge mansion that used to stand there," replied the CB. "This whole area up here on this plateau was a large banana plantation owned by some Frenchman. During the French-Indo-Chinese war the commies killed his family and burned him out. Just another of the casualties of war."

"Lord, that's a damn shame. I can see where this must have been a beautiful place before the Communists invaded it. I wouldn't mind settling in a place like this when I retire—providing it ever becomes peaceful and safe again."

"Yeah, this sure is some really exotic countryside, all right."

The power plant came into view as they rounded a turn in the winding mountain road and revealed mounds of twisted metal and broken pipes.

"Boy, Jacobs, you sure weren't kiddin' when you said they 'made a helluva mess' of the place." Roger remarked."

"No sh—t, Dick Tracy," Louie put in, "These CBs have a big job ahead on this project."

"Well, guys. **We've got a bit of work of our own** to do, to cover this the way it should be covered," Chief Gilmore advised the team. "Let's get to it and I want you to give me tak-son 'before' shots. Don't spare the film !"

The Chief had barely finished his instructions, when the Arriflex™ mopic cameras were buzzing and Seth began shooting the 'stills' he'd need to fill-in his stories.

The CBs and the cameramen were kept equally busy throughout the morning, and only took a brief breather at noon, when a truck from the camp brought them sandwiches and refreshments (one beer apiece).

"Beer for lunch ?" queried Louie. "I **LIKE** the way these CBs think."

"Don't get too carried away, Louie," the chief said, "You only get ONE, which is valuable, in this climate, to replace your body liquids and refresh you."

"Shucks, Chief, I don't drink **TOO MUCH** !"

"And, just how do you know when you've had **TOO MUCH** ?"

"When he **runs out of beer** !" Baldie shouted.

As the day progressed, the cameramen were all over the dam and power plant. By evening, they had exposed several hundred feet of movie film and enough 35mm Kodachrome™ to satisfy even Chief Gilmore's desires for 'Tak-Son' coverage.

"Fellas, I think you did a real day's work. We have a good start to this project and, with a couple more days of shooting repair pix, we might be able to 'wrap' this up in jig-time," the Chief advised the team.

"Man, these CBs really 'turn-and-burn' when they get goin'," Louie remarked, "At the rate they were going at it today, they'll have this plant spittin' volts and amps before the week's out!"

"Well," Jacobs said, "The quicker we finish the repairs, the quicker Saigon will have power 24/7. I know you guys got tired of the 'rollin' blackouts'. When you get back, you can put away the Coleman™ lanterns—at least until the VC hit us again."

At dinner that night, the CB Master Chief sat down with the photo crew and talked about the work ahead.

"You might be interested to know that tomorrow, we plan to clear the 'pad' for the new generator. After we finish doing that, we'll bring in the heavy crane and set the new generator in place. You should be able to get some real interesting shots when we do that. Then, all that's left is to hook up all the feed-lines and wiring—and then THROW THE SWITCH ! That'll bring the power from all four of the generators 'on-line' and Saigon will be fully ELECTRIFIED, again !"

Six

The project was going along like clock-work until the sirens blared a warning that *the VC were on the move*.

All work came to a halt and the CB camp quickly became a bee's nest of activity. Everyone, including the camera crew grabbed their weapons and headed for the nearest bunker.

The Marines threw the tarps off the howitzers and rammed home the 105mm projectiles, and stood by for firing. The three 'Ma-Deuce's' (M-2 .50 caliber heavy machine gun) were set up on their strategically located mounts and ammunition was passed out to the defenders.

Preparations were barely completed when the VC mortars began to announce the attack.

Initially, the mortar shells were falling short, but, with each explosion, the communist gunners were 'walking' the shells nearer and nearer the camp bunkers.

Chief Gilmore, Seth and Louie had dived into a bunker with two Marines who each had an M-79 (grenade launcher) as well as their AR-15 rifles. These,—along with the photographer's weapons—were putting out an impenetrable screen of firepower that staved off the VC in their sector.

Baldy and Roger were in another bunker, about thirty-yards away to the east, where three other Marines and a couple CBs were manning one of the M-2 .50 calibers, three AR-15s and Baldy's 'grease-gun' (a .45 caliber pistol-grip machine-gun).

The Marines, the CBs and photo team were managing to hold off the VC until about a dozen 'Charleys' made a screaming charge through the damaged main gate and were about to overrun the second perimeter bunkers. But the Marines in the first bunker hit them with a barrage of grenades and M-2 machine-gun fire, which put half of the attackers on the ground and the rest had second thoughts about charging into that hail of death.

The Communist troops kept up the pressure for two-and-a-half hours with charge after charge. Finally, dragging the bodies of their dead and wounded, they vanished into the trees and back to their mountain retreats.

When the *'All Clear'* sounded, a quick muster revealed one Marine seriously wounded during the charge through the gate, one CB with shrapnel in his lower-extremities, but no casualties among the camera crew—unless you count Louie getting dirt thrown in his face and eyes from an exploding mortar round which missed their bunker by about five-yards.

As things slowly returned to normal, Lt. Carson informed the Marine Staff Sergeant in charge of the Marines, that a 'skin-ship' (Med Evac Helo) was on it's way to pick up his wounded man and fly him to the nearest aid station for immediate treatment.

"My corpsman has him stabilized and advised me that he thought the medics there could patch him up and they'd be able to transport him to the Hospital Ship off Da Nang, where they can finish the job.," Lt. Cason assured the Sergeant.

"That's sure good to know, Lt. He's only two weeks away from rotation back to 'the world' I guess he'll be leaving a bit earlier than planned, but, at least it's not in a body-bag.".

"Amen to that, Sarge.".

"How about your guy, Lt.? Is he badly injured?"

"No, 'Doc', our corpsman, put him back in working shape with some tweezers and a couple of Band-Aids He'll be a little sore for a day or so, but, like you Marines, it takes more than that to put a CB down."

"Yeah, I had a chunk of shrapnel in my 'keester' a couple months ago, but I was back on the job two days later,:" Louie announced.

"And you cried and moaned every time you had to sit down," replied Seth.

"I didn't say it wasn't discomforting. Especially when we had to ride over some of these pot-hole trails that pass for 'roads' in this damn country."

"Incidentally, I hesitate to ask this—but did any of you camera jockeys **JUST HAPPEN** ro get any pictures in all the excitement?" was the Chief's inquiry.

"Yeah, Chief, what'd you think we came here for?" Baldy exploded, "I popped my head up several times and ran off a few feet of film. I made it short and sweet, though. 'Charlie' didn't get time to pick me off!"

"I ran off a few feet, too, but a lot of my shooting was the '**HAIL MARY'** method (holding the camera at arm's length overhead and aiming it by instinct)," Roger added, "I also took quite a bit of stuff on the men in my bunker, firing and loading."

"Chief, I think I got some pretty hot stuff of that charge through the gate," Louie said, "They were off to the left heading for the bunkers about twenty yards away so I was able to stand almost straight up, and got an excellent, unobstructed angle of the action. I guess I must have exposed over a hundred feet film on that charge."

"I managed to burn up about two rolls of 36 exposure Kodachrome™ between ducking and dodging all the 'incoming'," Seth added.

Chief Gilmore was also able to get some coverage, so between them they had a pretty good documentation of the battle

The following day there was work to be made up. 'Charlie' had set the repairs back several hours, so the CBs fell to their tasks and the film crew got back to documenting their efforts.

The placing and connecting of the new generator was ready to proceed after the CBs' had made up for most of the lost time.

"We're a half-a-day behind, Guys, but we'll still have this rig up and running sooner than Lt. Col. Egan had promised MACV, (the high US commander in Vietnam)," Lt. Carson praised his CBs, "You men have really shown the 'can do' spirit of all SeaBees."

By 1500 (3PM) the the following day, the generators were switched on for a test and, after everything checked out OK, with much ado and cheering from the entire CB camp, the generators were generatin' and power was '**back-on-line**' for Saigon and the suburbs.

There was much celebrating and back pounding in the CB's Club that night. Louie got his full ration of beer and managed to stay **moderately** sober. That's not saying that there were not a few CBs left with hangovers in the morning.

As dawn came, things began to get back to a somewhat normal level—not withstanding several aching heads and queazy stomachs.

"Well, Men," Lt. Carson addressed the photo-team, "I guess that about winds up your work here 'bouts. Let me know when you're ready and I'll set up transport back to Saigon for you."

"Lt., I think we might just stick around a day and get some 'home-towners' on your men," responded Chief Gilmore, "The people back 'state side' need to see that this party is not **ALL** shooting and bleeding. You deserve a whole lot of credit for what you do over here to improve the Vietnam life-style."

"That's aces with me and I know the men will be glad to cooperate in any way they can—even shave, if need be!"

Having finished their last-minute photo chores, the crew were transported back over the same rock and pot-hole strewn road to the postage-stamp air field in De Lat. There they had to wait because the C-47 encountered extreme head-winds. The same head-winds were to their advantage, though, returning to Saigon—pushing them along briskly and bringing them down at Tan Son Nhut Airport almost an hour ahead of their flight-plan schedule.

This required the men to pile their gear on the tarmac until they could find transport for it. Of course, as usual, Louie managed to solve the problem by 'commandeering' a baggage cart that was, to quote Louie—

"Just sitting there, not being used by anyone."

With all five men pushing and pulling they quickly got the camera gear to the front of the terminal and Louie was directed by Chief Gilmore to "get that thing back where you found it before anyone notices it's missing!"

Gilmore had phoned the Office letting them know of their unexpected arrival, so there was another delay while they waited for someone to pick them up. It was only a short time, though, until the van pulled up with Lt. Crocket acting chauffeur.

"Where's Teach?" the Chief inquired, "I figured he'd be the one to catch the driving duty."

"He and Lt. Duncan are over at the Army Hospital getting poked and prodded before they head state-side.," Lt. Crocket answered, "Teach is due to rotate back the same day as the Lt., and Teach thought he should have a complete physical before going home.

"You see, Teach's fifteen-year-old sister has a very weak immune system and he didn't wanted to be bringing home any virus or bug he might have picked up tromping through the Vietnamese jungles and swamps. Lt. Duncan was due for his annual anyway, so he's giving Teach moral support."

"That was nice of him," Seth commented.

"Personally, I think that sounds like a damn good move for all of us, before we return to 'The World'," Chief Gilmore observed, "There's no telling what kinda' maladies might be hitchin' a ride in our bodies."

"Amen, to that," commented the rest of the team.

"OK, Men. Let's unload the gear in the office for the night. You can come back in the morning to clean it up and prepare for the next project," Lt. Crocket ordered, "We don't have any jobs lined up for a couple days. That'll give us time to plan what kind of 'send off' we should throw for Lt. Duncan and Teach."

"We gotta' make it a GOOD ONE, Guys," Louie suggested," They've both been watching our 'six' while we gallivanted 'round Asia and had all the 'fun'(?). We wouldn't have the comfortable 'digs' if it hadn't been for the Lt., and teach managed to take care of our travelin' orders and keep the rent on the Villa paid up. We owe them a REAL SHINDIG. Agreed?"

"Passed, and so ordered," the Chief followed up.

Most of the crew opted for a good night's rest and stayed in the Villa in lieu of any bar-hopping, etc. All that most wanted, was to have a good meal at the NCO Club and to 'hit the sack'.

The following two days was spent leisurely doing gear maintenance, getting the data sheets and film ready, for shipment and recuperating from the power plant job.

Teach's replacement, Storekeeper Second George Cox, had reported aboard and Teach spent the time bringing him 'up to speed' on the operation of the Villa and the other duties of the 'rear guard'.

Lt. Duncan and Teach were booked on a flight to Tachikawa AFB in Japan, early Monday morning to make connection with their flight back to the US of A. So the plans for the 'going away' party were number one priority on the men's 'to do' list.

They all voted to have it at 'The Victory' restaurant, and, since Roger was getting more and more fluent in the 'lingo', he was assigned to take charge of working with the restaurant's chef in choosing the menu, etc.

"It'll HAVE to be Saturday night to give them time to recover from the festivities before take-off Monday." Lt. Crocket suggested.

"That's for damn sure," Baldy agreed, "I've tried flying after a night 'on the town' and it ain't no fun with a hangover!"

"OK, That's settled, then. Roger, you, Baldy and Louie will work out the details with the able assistance of Chief Gilmore. Whatever you need to make everything right, Call on me and I'll 'jack-up' some of my connections. I can get steaks etc, if you want. Just name it!" Lt. Crocket told the crew.

"What I can't scrounge up, Lt. ain't in Vietnam," Louie bragged.

"**Believe him, Lt.** If Louie can't get it, it ain't to be got!" affirmed Seth.

Besides steaks and mushrooms, the chef had come up with ***Chagio*** (VN spring rolls), ***Pho*** (beef-noodle soup) ***C a' ha'p*** (steamed fish) and three or four other Vietnamese delicacies. To wash it down, there was a couple of cases of ***Ba Me Ba*** (#33 beer) and several bottles of fine rice wine.

To top off the meal, the restaurant also provided music from a string-quartet plinking on the Vietnamese versions of guitar and fiddle.

When the festivities were over, all hands agreed it'd been 'some shindig'.

Sunday was a day of R & R with little or no activity from the abused and suffering bodies.

Monday everyone piled out at the crack of dawn to give Lt Duncan and Teach a **REAL NAVY** sendoff of a wish for—***FAIR WINDS AND FOLLWING SEAS !!***

SEVEN

After the party, a calm had set in and then, true to form, **ALL HELL** broke loose up north in **I Corps.**

"We have our new 'marching orders', gentlemen," Lt Crocket announced to the troops, "There are several small villages west of Da Nang that are being terrorized by VC attacks. 'Charlie' is murdering and burning in retaliation for the anti-communist leaning of the villagers. They've killed dozens of people—even infants and grandmothers—in their furtive attempt to eradicate them. Our Marines are staging a huge S & D' (search and destroy) sweep of the area to drive out the VC.

"We'll be providing saturation coverage of the VC's destruction, and, hopefully, be able to document the Marine rescue of the remaining villagers.

"Go prepared to witness horrific brutality. You haven't seen anything as bad as they're reporting from I Corps. Those Commies are inhuman animals. They slaughtered those innocent people just because they resisted their ideology."

"Lt., I could have told you they're sumbitch butchers. I spent time as a POW in Korea and I've witnessed it, FIRST HAND! Ain't no difference between a North Korean Commie and a North Vietnamese Commie!" Chief Gilmore stated, "Take it from me, they're not human!"

"There you have it men. Right from 'the voice of experience' ! Steel yourselves for a rough job.

"Now, gather the gear you'll need for three days. Chief, you and Baldy will be with the Marines conducting the search and destroy mission, so keep your 'baggage' light," Lt. Crocket directed, "You'll be moving fast and quiet.

"Seth, you, Louie and Roger have the tough job of covering a USO group coming to entertain the troops in Da Nang and a couple other bases in the area. They'll also be visiting with patients in the Da Nang Hospital which is <u>priority one</u> on their tour. Com Med wants **lots and lots** of audience reactions, laughing, cheering, etc. Where possible, get names and home-towns. It ain't gonna' be all roses and it'll keep you hoppin' to get the coverage necessary to make a proper 'show' of it. Let's make a **CCG production** that'll please Washington."

"Got the 'plan', Lt.," Seth said, "We'll bring back pix and a story to swell the hearts of these guys' families back in 'The World'."

"That's the ol' CCG spirit, Men."

The team had only four hours to get organized and board their Air Commando C-130 aircraft carrying them north to Da Nang. Conversation and light banter was a no-no. This was an 'all-hands', 'all-business' evolution. No time for fun and games.

In Da Nang the group split up—the Chief and Baldy, off to rendezvous with the Marine Assault Force.—Seth and his group to the **I-Corp** Press tent to make connections to set up their USO project.

Hooking up with their Marine driver, Gilmore and Baldy were whisked off to the Marine Third MAF Forward Command HQ. There they were given a quick briefing and ordered to form up to move out in fifteen minutes.

"Chief, they sure don't allow a fella' much time to catch a breather, do they?" Bald observed.

"All the more better, Son. It also doesn't allow much room for building up the tension of waiting."

The Marine Lt. Col. gave them a final warning about silence and staying on EXTREME ALERT.

"The purpose of these missions is to rescue the villagers and annihilate or drive off the VC. As with any conflict, we want you all to return safe. So keep your eyes and ears open—watch out for snipers and 'boobie-traps'. They've been in those villages and surrounding jungles long enough to plant plenty of them! Shove off and GOD BE WITH YOU!"

The two photographers and ten Marines slung their gear and moved off into the tree-line.

The first village they came upon was nothing but charred remains with no one in sight. They deployed around the area and searched for signs of which way the VC were headed and where they were liable to hit next. The Marine Sergeant in charge of the force gathered his men and pointed on his map to a village nearby.

"I'd bet my stripes that's their next target," he said, "Let's hope we're in time to catch them in the act. I don't know where these villagers have gone but, we didn't find any bodies so, hopefully they 'di-di' ed out before 'Charlie' struck.

"Come on men, let's play **'TOM'** to their **'JERRY'** and see if we can sneak up on them."

"MEOW," uttered one of the Marine Privates,

"QUIET, wise-guy. Starting right now, anything you people have to say, that isn't an emergency, keep your mouths sealed."

Their movement was slow, deliberate and silent from that point.

As they neared the target village they spread out in an encircling move to cut off the VC escape when the shooting started. Two of the huts had already been torched and four VC with fire brands in the hands were headed for the larger dwelling. That's when the command was given to the Marines to 'GREASE 'EM'.

The air was filled with the thunder of weapon-fire and grenades exploding. The surprise was successful and the VC were caught completely off guard. The ones with the fire brands in their hands had laid down their weapons to carry out their arson intentions—BIG MISTAKE—they were the first to go down.

The women and children were screaming and yelling and running every which way. The scene was complete pandemonium.

Suddenly, Baldy was seen to lay down his Arriflex™ movie camera and go charging into one of the burning huts. Chief Gilmore turned his camera just in time to catching Baldy's action on film. He caught a fleeting glimpse of Baldy diving through the flaming doorway.

"OH MY GOD," He exclaimed," **He'll be burned to a crisp.**"

The words had barely cleared his lips, when Baldy came rolling out of the thatch hut clutching a wad of clothes in his arms.

"WHAT IN HELL DID YOU THINK YOU WERE DOING? YOU HAIRY GOOFBALLL." Chief Gilmore scolded him.

"Chief, As I was busy filming, I heard somebody in that hooch crying and just couldn't stand idle and let them die."

As Baldy spoke he pulled back the wad of clothes he had been clutching, and revealed a small infant not more than a year to a year-and-a-half old, smiling and gurgling.

"I'll be Damned," the Marine Sergeant marveled, "I've seen everything now. I'm going to see that you get a commendation for that!"

"And I'll second that!!" Gilmore said.

"Shucks, Chief, I only did what any one of these men would have done under the same circumstances. I just happened to be the one closest to that burning hooch. I don't need no 'glory badge' for savin' that little tyke. Just to see his smile is all the reward I need."

"Well, I'm not going to forget it," the Chief replied, "And I got it on film, just to prove it."

"At least, Chief, I don't think I'll have to shave my head for a while. I singed it down to my scalp. Surprising though, I don't think it cooked any skin."

"Thank GOD for small favors," the Chief marveled.

The Marines did what they could to put out the fires and salvage the rest of the Vietnamese village and get the people calmed down and back to their lives. With things back to normal—well, **almost**—the men set off to try to find the VC and end the attacks on the innocent peasants.

It seemed the VC had had enough, though, and had crawled back into their holes, for now at least. There was nothing more the Marines could do. The VC had left no trail so they headed back to the Third MAF HQ.

Seth and his team had a busy time of it too. No violence or dodging bullets, but, exciting enough to keep them on their toes trying to get on film all the entertainment provided by the USO troop and the reception given them by the appreciative audiences of servicemen.

At one of the camps on the USO tour, Seth, Roger and Louie had done their usual splitting up of the area of coverage and were proceeding with their filming.

Louie was 'working' the stage getting close-ups of the entertainers and scenes of the audience, when he was suddenly grabbed from behind and swung into the arms of one of the the NFL Cheerleader beauties and found himself doing the 'jitter bug' in front of several hundred cheering men.

"GO, MAN,GO !! The mob screamed.

Louie regained his composure and began enjoying the spotlight. As the music finished, Louie was rewarded with a **KISS** from his dancing partner initiating <u>more</u> cheers from the onlookers.

At the end of the day Louie was as much a celebrity as the members of the USO troop.

"I guess there'll be no livin' with him from now on," Roger observed.

"Don't I know it," replied Seth.

Two more camps and then it was off to the Da Nang Hospital.

There the troop was given a reception that over-shadowed those they had received at the previous stops on the tour.

The CBs had constructed a near-professional stage with lights and buntings to provide a very theatrical setting for the entertainers.

The Medical CO set up a formal reception dinner for the troop and spread a table unseen in Vietnam for decades. Seth and his crew were kept busy trying to cover all the festivities and the **BIG SHEW !** that the troop put on the following afternoon.

The next day the USO people departed for Saigon and their return to 'the world'. The CCG team finished shipping the film and stories and declared this project finished ! Now it was back to Tan Son Nhut and the next one.

EIGHT

The afternoon after their return the Villa had visitors.

An Army jeep pulled up to the gate with two MPs in it and Louie seated in the back seat.

One of the MPs got out and yanked the chain attached to the bell hanging on the gate-post.

Lt. Crocket and Seth, weapons in hand, answered the ring.

"Lt., is this one of your men?" the Army Corporal at the gate asked.

"Yes. He's one of my cameramen, What's this all about?"

"Well, Sir, we picked him up outside the Cho Lon Military Exchange with contraband he had purchased. The merchandise was obviously not for his personal use but was destined for the 'Black Market'."

"What did he have, Corporal?" Lt. Crocket asked.

"Sir, he had four cases of Tampons™, two cases of Kotex™ and a dozen nylon stockings in his bag and was hailing a 'Cyclo' when we apprehended him."

"I see what you mean about 'personal use'. Louie, is this true?"

"Yes, Lt. But I can explain. You see, I was taking them to some of the Vietnam nurses at the Saigon Army Hospital. They can't get these things except on the 'Black Market' and they're too damn expensive there, so I was bringing this stuff as a gift for them. They treated me real nice when I was working there. I just wanted to do something for them as a 'thank you' gift"

"Whether that was your motive, or not, that's where they're going. Corporal, I'll take responsibility for this man. His story could be true— as ridiculous as it may seem."

Louie insisted it was a fact. His 'penance' for his 'fuel-up foul-up' did lend a bit of credence to his story.

"If you say so, Lt. We've had so much 'Black Market' stuff on the streets that our Provost Marshal boss is making us crack down on any suspicious activity."

"Thanks, Corporal. I'll make sure my man follows through on his claimed 'gift' intentions. Have a good evening."

Returning to the Villa, the Lt. instructed Seth:

"First thing in the morning, Seth, I want you to personally escort this Cajon over to the Hospital and watch him make his presentation!"

"Aye, Aye, Sir."

Another day passed before the CCG team was called to action again. This time it was a group of CBs at Chu Lai who were deserving of the 'Crazy Camera Guys' full treatment.

"These eight SeaBees are in charge of guiding LSTs and small-craft to the beach at Chu Lai to unload ammo and supplies for **I-Corps**," the 7th Fleet Operations Officer informed the men, "Their job is vital as it over-rides the need for all this logistics having to be trucked down from the Da Nang port. Too many of the convoys have been 'high-jacked' and needed supplies come up short."

"I can see the importance of their work, Jerry, and we'll get on it right away." Lt. Crocket assured him.

"Chief, I want you, Seth and Louie to hop the next flight north. I have another assignment for Baldy and Roger down in the Mekong Delta.

"This should keep all of you busy and out of mischief for a few days," the Lt. said, relief in his voice.

"While you're out of the way Petty Officer Cox and I will be spending our time getting all the 'Action Reports' and rental accounts in order. Don't forget—rent's due the end of the month."

"I just hope I have enough to bail me out," Baldy remarked, "My Sainted Mother always preached to me to, 'Save your money for a rainy day' but all this monsoon rain we've been getting has got me about broke !"

"Well, Baldy, if you can't come up with your rent, we'll just have to take it out of your hairy hide," Chief Gilmore assured him.

With that the light banter came to a halt and all hands started hustling together the gear they would need for their projects.

Since only the Delta job might encounter shooting, Seth and Louie were going lightly armed on their deployment to Chu Lai. Baldy and Roger, on the other hand were to accompany a team of SEALs into the swamps on an intelligence gathering mission. Stealth was required for this and—it was hoped—no contact with the enemy force would make shooting necessary.

"They'll be locating VC camps and strongholds down there and mapping them out for future targets," the 7th Fleet Ops Officer warned the men, "It's important the enemy doesn't even know you've been in their vicinity. So keep alert but refrain from using your weapons unless **ABSOLUTELY NECESSARY !"**

"Understood, Lt.," Baldy said, "Don't shoot 'til you 'see the whites of their eyes'—and only then if those eyes are looking at you over the sites of a weapon."

"That's one way of putting it, Sailor,"

The road to the SEAL team's lair was a one lane ox-cart trail with a river on the left and a rice paddy on the right. There was an occasional wide spot allowing pull-off when meeting oncoming traffic thus averting accidents—usually !

After 3-4 clicks (kilometers) the river bank became a dense jungle of underbrush, palmetto and large trees. Hidden under the overhanging trees and vines was the barge which served the SEALs as bunkhouse, kitchen and secure storage for weapons of various calibers and death dealing effectiveness

Over the door to the barge was a sign, neatly printed in RED, saying:

"YEAH, THOUGH I WALK THROUGH THE VALLEY OF THE SHADOW OF DEATH, I FEAR NO EVIL, *FOR I AM THE MEANEST BASTARD IN THE VALLEY ! !*

The SEALs were feared by Viet Cong <u>and</u> the North Vietnamese Army. They called them the 'devils with green faces' and 'meat eaters'. Enemy forces avoided contact with them at all costs !

The SEALs out-did the Green Berets, in that, besides doing everything those Special Forces could do, they were trained to fight in the water as well as parachute into the battle zone A more than 'triple threat' combination.

"You photo-mates get your gear ready to go," the senior SEAL told them, "We'll be boarding that PRB (high speed shallow-water boat) at 2330 hours (11:30 PM) and heading up the river under cover of darkness. I hope you guys can get pictures under limited light conditions. We can't let them even suspect we're anywhere around.

"Our undercover Vietnamese informants report the VC seem very sure of their positions and have very lax security deployed outside the actual compound. We need to get a head-count and, try to ascertain their weaponry. This means **ABSOLUTE SILENCE and STEALTH**! We're not here to engage in any fire-fight, just to 'get the facts, Mam' as Joe Friday would say."

In the pitch-black night, the PBR got underway towing two modified Zodiac. rubber rafts.

The modifications were made especially for the SEALs operations. They included: constructing the craft of a Kevlar™ and rubber fabric making the rafts almost puncture-proof. The Zodiacs were also propelled by 'souped-up' electric motors thus almost eliminating any motor noise. Each raft could accommodate four men in prone position putting three SEALs and a photographer in each.

"We're going into the Nam Cam Forest where the Commies have taken their positions," the men were informed by the SEAL Leader, "We'll have a ways to hike so be alert for 'trip wires', 'pungee sticks' and any other form of 'boobie-traps'." he warned.

"What's a 'pungee stick'," Baldy inquired.

"These bastards like to sharpen a piece of bamboo, dip it in excrement and plant them aling the trails. Step on one or get scratched and it's **INSTANT** INFECTION !" was his dire warning.

"Geez, that's 'dirty' pool, don't you think?"

"As they say, 'All's fair in love and war, and the VC and I don't see this as LOVE !'"

"OK. We're about one click from our landing point, so, everybody into the Zodiacs, and no talking from here on—only hand signals."

The SEAL at the tiller of the lead Zodiac guided it slowly and silently up the river to the point where they aimed to make their landing. So far there was no indication that they had been discovered.

The men slipped silently into the shallow water and dragged the raft further onto the shore and covered it with palmetto branches. The second Zodiac landed a few feet away and was also swiftly concealed from discovery by any passing boats or prowling VC.

The suspected enemy encampment was several yards into the jungle so the SEAL observers were forced to 'snake crawl' to get near enough to study and record the Communist resources and manpower. The village was a shambles and proved to be abandoned. All the huts had been burned to the ground but no bodies were found. A slow, encircling-sweep around the compound to seek out any lurking 'Charlies' and the Lead SEAL signaled to *'pull back !'*

As swiftly as they had arrived, the SEALs melted back into the dense jungle and began their advance further into the underbrush to their second target. No words were uttered and all movement was directed by well-rehearsed hand signals.

Baldy and Roger, not well-versed in the SEAL hand code, just closely watched what their SEAL Team buddies were doing and followed suit Baldy later remarked, "We just played 'Monkey **SEE**—Monkey **DO**'!"

The advance on the second camp caught the VC completely off guard. When they got close enough they could see that 'Charlie' had apparently had a little 'drinking party' and all appeared to be in a drunken coma. Even the two sentries had laid aside their weapons and were snoozing.

The SEALs took full advantage of the enemy condition and, still moving silently—so as not to arouse the sleepyheads—they proceeded to examine and gather every scrap of paper that even resembled a map or 'Op Order'. It appeared they had gathered enough information to cripple the Communists plans for months.

The Lead SEAL, waved his hand in a sweeping circle over his head which all knew meant:

"LET'S 'Di-Di Mau' OUR OF HERE !"

Their withdrawal was going well when—***CRACK!*** It was the distinct sound of an AK-47

"Hit the dirt !" the man 'on-point' hoarsely whispered.

"Is anyone hit? I couldn't tell where that came from so everyone keep you eyes open, your butts down and let's try to ease back to the boats."

No further shots were heard so the raiding party uncovered their Zodiacs and charged full speed down to their rendezvous with the PBR. As the sun began to wipe away the black of the night they were swooping down the river for 'home'.

The outstanding success of the operation put everyone in a joyous mood, but they would have to hold their shouting and celebrating 'til they were further down the river and nearing home—no sense inviting trouble.

Chief Gilmore, Serh and Louie arrived at Chu Lai early in the afternoon and were met at the small air strip by the Beach Master, Senior Chief Patrick Logan.

"Welcome, men," was the Senior Chief's greeting, "This ain't much of a 'base' but we call it 'hell away from home'. We're on a break right now. We operate with the tides.

"The next high tide is at 0723 (7:23 AM) and that's when we start bringing in the barges. They load off-shore from the cargo ships and then are herded to the beach by 'mules'—not the four legged kind—they're actually just a 500 horse-power Marine Engine mounted on a floating raft. Our job is to get the barges as far onto the shore as possible then tie them off to those poles sunk into the solid ground. They're off-loaded there and will remain high-and-dry until the afternoon tide refloats them.

"So you guys get settled in, get a good night's rest and we'll be up and ready to 'rock-and-roll' at 0500."

The SeaBees were also responsible for maintaining the mooring gear and keeping the 'road ?' from the landing zone in repair—no mean task—with the heavy trucks passing over it and the monsoon rains turning it into a marshland almost every day.

As dawn comes, it appears this is going to be one of those wet days. The winds were beginning to pick up and the monsoon rain was starting a gentle downpour.

"You Guys are going to see just how hairy this operation can be, today." Logan warned the cameramen, "The seas are getting choppy and these barges are as hard to herd as a bunch of elephants. Keep awake and **STAY OUTSIDE THE MOORING LINES** ! They can snap and cut a body in half.

"So far we've had one part and swing around like a 'bull-whip'. Luckily no one was caught in it's swath."

"I, for one, would like to keep my skin in one piece," Louie remarked, "I know my body isn't worth more than about 98 cents but I kind of prefer it just as it is."

"You and me both, Lil' Buddy," Seth agreed.

"On to the job at hand," Chief Gilmore cut in, "We're going to be fighting the wind, rain and limited light to get any coverage, so carry only high speed film and plenty of plastic to keep your gear dry."

"Chief, I was out scouting the weather and encountered the damndest phenomena I ever ran into," Seth reported, "The rain had turned the ground along the road into quicksand. I was thigh-deep in mud trying to struggle back to solid ground while, at the same time, dust and sand was blowing into my face."

"We get that a lot, Son," Senior Chief Logan laughed, "This is a strange, strange world. Every day it gets curiouser, and curiouser."

The first barge was approaching the beach as the sun came up. The swells were growing larger and larger by the minute and the beach workers were frantically struggling to get the lines tied to the anchor-poles on the shore. They completed the job of securing the first craft, when the second came bounding off a huge wave and landed high dry sideways on the sand.

"DAMN IT !" Logan shouted, "That's sure going to ruin our day. It'll take both bull-dozers and all four of the 'mules' to get that sumbitch squared away and ready to ride the afternoon tide back to sea !"

Logan's First Class Rigger and the other SeaBees furiously tugged the tie-down ropes to their anchor poles and began the task of getting the cargo unloaded onto waiting trucks.

"With all the weight off those barges, it'll make it a hell of a lot easier to maneuver them back afloat again, at least." Senior Chief Logan said with relief.

As it turned out, the afternoon tide was a bit higher than usual, making the recovery operation go better than had been anticipated.

"Man, oh man, Chief," Louie laughingly remarked, "With all the problems with that damn barge and all, I think I got some terrific footage. It was bad luck for these SEABees but **DAMN GOOD f**er picher takin'. We couldn't have staged it any better to heighten the excitement of the moment"

"I guess, between your angle and my cross-angle we did OK. It's too bad the Bees had such a time of it, but, I'd say 'all's well that ends well'. I think we ought to be able to wrap this one after we get some 'cut-in' facial close-ups, in the morning," Gilmore remarked.

"I got some real good sound recording of the waves breaking and the shouting during the struggle," Seth added, "That should really set the scene."

All the men were exhausted and hit the sack early without any further banter. Too beat to make jokes or complain about the day's events.

In the morning, Chief Gilmore and Louie shot several 'one-ups' of all the SeaBees' faces while Seth recorded their comments to tape. By late morning the project was declared finished and the CCG team packed up for the trip back to Saigon.

The monsoon had abated, leaving Chu Lai a quagmire of saturated mud but the air strip, being covered with steel matting, was still usable, so the daily Da Nang to Saigon Courier flight was able to pick up the cameramen and return them to their Saigon 'home-away-from-home'.

Back at the Tan Son Nhut office, the Lt. and Petty Officer Cox had completed their task of sorting out and forwarding to San Diego HQ the paper-work and had brought the rent records up to date. So a two-day stand down was declared for the troops to catch their breaths and recharge their batteries—both physical and photographic.

"You Guys are three lucky bastards. The 7th Fleet office just got the word that the night after you left, the Chu Lai SeaBee compound was hit," Lt. Crocket announced to Chief Gilmore, Seth and Louie, "One of the CBs was killed and two were wounded. Senior Chief Logan and the rest of his crew managed to 'grease' six VC and drove off the remaining dozen or so.

"They called in a MedEvac Helo that rushed the two wounded to the Da Nang hospital where the docs say they're going to be OK. Second Class Bos'n's Mate Hank Carter was killed instantly when he fell on a grenade at the outset of the battle. They say the grenade would have taken out about half the SeaBee force, but for Carter's sacrifice.".

"They say there's a thin line between foolishness and heroism, but this was **BRAVERY !** in any man's language !" Seth pronounced.

NINE

The first day of the 'stand-down' went by with hardly a 'peep' out of anyone. They were too pooped to do much talking—or even move. from their bunks—the Villa was silent. The town around them was still bustling with it's usual beeping of the horns and the roaring of the cyclos, the motorcycles, the smoke-belching trucks and taxis.

At 1:00 AM, however, the quiet was torn apart by a large **EXPLOSION** nearby. By training and instinct of preservation, the entire populous of the Villa grabbed their weapons and their flak-vests and dove under bunks or tables for cover.

"What in GOD's name was that?" Petty Officer Cox exclaimed from his position under two mattresses.

"That was 'Charlie's' usual harassing 'wakey wakey' call," replied Baldy. "However, his mortars don't very often reach this far into the city. He must have sneaked his weapon past the city's perimeter check-points to be able to throw his little greeting-cards into our neighborhood."

The men waited to hear the rattle of gunfire that usually followed 'Charlie's' shenanigans but, this time there nothing but silence but for the low babble of the Vietnamese shop keepers and residents complaining of the damage to their property. There apparently were no casualties and the Com Sat (VN police) went about their job of trying to locate the inconsiderate bastard who would wake people at this time of the morning

"Just life in beautiful downtown Saigon," commented Seth, "The 'Pearl of the Orient'."

"I don't know about the rest of you turkey-necks, but I'm gonna' have me a beer to calm my nerves," Baldy announced, "Gettin' rousted out of the first good night's sleep I've had in weeks has kinda' jangled my thinking'."

The whole crew agreed with Baldy's suggestion and trooped down to the living room while Baldy retrieved the picnic cooler of beer from the kitchen.

Seth had just popped the first top, when Chief Gilmore came in.

"I stepped outside to check the situation and learned that it wasn't a mortar that blasted us out of our sleep. Some Commie on a Vespa™ had cruised by and tossed a small satchel charge in the doorway of a Villa just three doors down. They apparently found out five Army CID agents had rented an apartment there. They obviously didn't get all their sh—t straight though cause the agents had rented the apartment on the **second floor** in **the rear of the building,** and barely heard the explosion.

"All I've got to say about that is—it was **STILL TOO DAMN CLOSE FOR COMFORT,**" Roger commented, "I'm sweatin' it that our Villa could be next. You know the VC have put a 1000 piastre reward on the heads of all U.S. news media—which includes **US!**"

"You would have to bring up that sweet little bit of info, Roger!" Louie admonished him, "now I **WON'T** be able to get back to sleep!"

"If we just don't flaunt the fact we're camera jockeys, and keep a low profile, we shouldn't be in much more danger than when we're out on patrol with the Marines or SEALs," Lt Crocket assured them, "Now, let's can all the chatter. Put your weapons on 'safety' and climb back into the sack for some sleep!"

Day two of their 'stand down' was without further excitement. The team spent their 'down time' getting their equipment ready for whatever future escapades were in store.

"That Chu Lai job pushed our cameras and sound gear through hell," moaned Seth, "That monsoon rain and then the blowing sand means a complete breakdown and cleaning. That'll take care of any 'time off' today."

"I think all of the gear could use a thorough going over and testing," Chief Gilmore added, "It's ain't good to get out in the jungle and have a malfunction, cameras or weapons."

All hands turned to getting the job done so they might still have some time left to relax.

They didn't have to wait long for their next assignments. When they returned, well rested, to the office the 7th Fleet Ops Officer was waiting to talk to Lt. Crocket.

"A gigantic engagement is starting up in the E Drang Valley and we need all the coverage your team can provide," he told the Lt., "We've committed hundreds of troops into this operation and they're meeting tremendous enemy resistance. Casualties are already heavy, so your men will be in extreme danger. Be sure they all wear their flak-vests and helmets and proceed with maximum caution."

"Jerry, you don't need to worry about my guys. They're pretty 'seasoned' to combat by now. My team will get all the documentation you can possibly need and come back, **GOD WILLING!** with their skins intact."

"Lt., I know they'll carry out their job, and I pray they **DO** come back safely. Their movies and stills will be a historical record for future generations to see what this war is all about. Good luck, men, may you have **'FAIR WINDS AND FOLLOWING SEAS'!"**

"You all got the 'word' and know what to expect," Lt. Crocket spoke to the men, "One word of advise, avoid filming the dying and suffering—the civilian media already overdoes that—concentrate, instead, on the heroism and dedication to duty of these troops. They deserve better for their sacrifices."

The cameramen were helo'd to the forward command post from which the battle was being directed. There they were assigned to the squads they'd be accompanying into battle.

"OK, you Mugs," Chief Gilmore told them before they took off in their separate directions, "Keep your butts down and those cameras rollin' and I pray we ALL can have a few beers together when this sh—t is over!"

"AMEN," was the collective reply from the team.

There was no time for hesitation. Everyone quickly took off to get the job done. Even on the move, Seth was busy shooting stills and asking men for names and hometowns.

His big job was to write the stories of these men and to convey their courage and sacrifice to the families back home by word and picture.

The rest of the team was also busy filming the troops' movement through the jungle, heading into the fray. The tense faces of young men walking into the 'shadow of death'. Everyone was silently anticipating what lay ahead.—would they survive, be wounded or, GOD forbid, meet death in this land thousands of miles from home.

Gilmore's squad was the first to come under fire.

"Hit the deck, We've got contact!" the squad leader yelled.

The cracking of rifle-fire and mortar shells exploding in the nearby brush brought everyone into fighting mode. The Chief snake-crawled behind a fallen palm log for cover and began firing his AR-15 with one hand and trying to capture the action on film with the other.

A second squad fell in beside the embattled first squad and all were pouring fire onto the enemy positions, mowing down the dense brush and many of the enemy who were using the brush for concealment. The intense fighting ceased. after about fifteen minutes and the jungle grew silent, except for the far off sounds of other battles raging in the distant reaches of the jungle.

Chief Gilmore's group had sustained only two minor injuries. The two were treated by the Navy Medic and escorted back to the CP. The rest of the two squads began to again move forward, on full alert for any more sign of the enemy.

Seth's Marines had moved deeper into the jungle without encountering resistance. Baldy's had run into a small force and eliminated those that didn't 'di-di mau' quickly to other places. Roger's force had to fight their way out of an ambush which the squad's point-man spotted an instant before the enemy was able to spring the trap. They met the VC attack with a withering fusillade of rifle, machinegun and RPG (rocket-propelled-grenade launcher) fire. The enemy melted under such resistance and, after losing over half of their force, decided to pull back, dragging their dead and wounded with them.

The battles continued for two days and two nights with heavy casualties on both sides. The VC were later judged to have lost several thousand and the ARVN (South Vietnamese Army) and U.S. forces suffered dishearteningly large losses as well. All over a measly 70 or 80 acres of rice paddies and jungle.

On the second day of the fighting, the U.S. Force Commander ordered our forces to pull back 500 yards and called in aircraft with napalm to **'SMOKE 'EM OUT !'**

This finally broke the VC command and they quickly snaked back into the jungle to 'lick their wounds'. The VC withdrawal left the U.S troops nothing to do but carry their wounded back to the CP and gather up the weapons left on the battlefield.

Back at the CP, Baldy, of course, had a tale to tell to all who would listen.

"I was busy getting some outstanding footage of the U.S. and ARVN troops beside me blasting away at 'Charlie', when a sniper off to my right rang my bell with a ricochet off my helmet ! I saw stars and was sure I heard 'Big Ben' chime 'one-o'clock'," Baldy bragged, "Look here, you can see the dent that mutha put in my nice new helmet."

"You're just damn lucky that 'dent' isn't in your nice bald head," Gilmore scolded him, "Next time, keep your f—kin' head down. You might not be so lucky again."

"Well, that particular sniper won't get another chance. The Sarge with me, took his BAR and blew the top of that palm to smithereens along with the 'monkey' hiding in it !"

"Hoorah !" shouted Louie.

"I'll **'HOORAH'** ! ! to that, too," added Seth.

R &R—A day of Rest and Relaxation and it was back to work.

Lt. Crocket returned to the office from his 7th Fleet Operations morning briefing with news of the team's next assignment.

"You guys best get your 'sea-legs' back in shape," he announced, "CinCPac wants you to give the 'royal treatment' to the people on the ships that are supporting this war from the South China Sea. So far, they haven't gotten a whole lot of credit by the media. It's time we give them 'the ol' CCG treatment'. So stock up on the seasick pills and break out your sea-going duds.

"You'll all be picked up by the USS 'Tico' (Ticonderado) COD (Carrier On-board Delivery S-2 aircraft) first thing in the morning. They'll fly you out to the 'Tico'. From there you, Seth, Louie and Baldy will be hi-lined over to three other ships of the task force. Chief and Roger will remain on the carrier.

"You're going to be operating on your own, so put on your thinkin' caps and make their families proud."

"Hey, Lt., I think this is a great idea," Roger commented, "Those sea-going 'Swabbies' work some pretty long hours and they're stuck out there on the water with little, or no liberty. I know, from my short ten months of sea duty, that it's a pretty boring, thankless life."

Landing on the pitching flight-deck of a carrier in the middle of the China Sea was a new experience for the photo team. Except for Chief Gilmore. In his 25 years of service, he had logged dozens of launches and recoveries, so he tried to prepare his men for this new and most unusual event.

"Snug-up your seat-belts and shoulder harnesses, put your head down and clasp your fingers behind your head. As the plane touches down it will, hopefully, snag the arresting gear cable, at which time the pilot will 'reverse-pitch' and the plane will cease it's forward motion," Gilmore instructed the cameramen, "The aircraft will go from about 225 mph to **ZERO** in a fraction of a second. It'll feel like riding the front seat of a Mac truck and hitting a brick wall at 100 mph. No one who followed these instructions has suffered anything more than two shaky legs when they walked away."

"Chief," Louie enquired, "All I see down there is a little row boat. Where's the ship?"

"That **IS THE SHIP** ! Louie," was his answer, "It's going to appear tiny right up to about the time we touch down. Don't worry, though, these Navy pilots seldom miss the deck!"

"WELL, I'm saying an extra 'Hail Mary' until I have my feet firmly planted on that floating 'bird-farm'!"

"Can't hurt!"

"STAND BY FOR LANDING," the pilot warned.

With a tremendous jolt, the plane was down and the whole team, having held their breaths, let out a loud chorus of sighs.

"Jeeze," Baldy exclaimed, "I thought my nuts were going to come out my mouth!"

TEN

Lt.jg Butterfield, the 'Tico's' Public Affairs Officer, met the photographers as they disembarked from the COD aircraft.

"I understand two of you men will remain aboard and we need to hi-line or helo the others to other ships in the task-force. I've made berthing arrangements for you, Chief, in the Chief's quarters and Petty Officer you'll bunk in the OP Division quarters with the ship's Photogs and JOs (journalists).

"I've assigned Journalist First Class Owens to be your liaison aboard 'Tico'. He's been on board longer than any of my other staff, so he can expedite your navigating around the ship. Anything you need, just ask. We've been instructed by CinCPac to give you the 'red carpet' treatment."

"Thanks, Lt.," the Chief said, "We'll try not to disrupt things any more than necessary. I presume we can stow our camera gear in the ship's photo lab?"

"No problem, Chief. The lab chief has been briefed and is expecting you. We'll be helo-ing two of your men to a Destroyer and a Destroyer Escort this afternoon. The other one will be hi-lined to an AKA supply ship that'll be coming alongside at 0800 (8:AM) in the morning. He can bunk down for the night with our photographers, but be ready with his gear and standing by on the starboard aircraft elevator at 0730.

The camera crew was still shaken up and rubber-legged after their first experience with landing aboard a carrier.

"I kid you not," Louie commented, "I ain't never been that scared since I came under my first enemy fire up in Pleiku!"

"Yeah, I heard how you wet your britches that time, Louie," Baldy teased.

"It wasn't as bad as it could have been though. I was hip deep in a rice paddy when it happened so it didn't show. The poor farmer, however, sure had a salty rice crop that season!" chuckled Louie.

'Incidentally, Louie, I noticed, when I was getting our orders endorsed, that they have your first name as 'LEROY'. What's the story?" Seth inquired.

"'The story' is—when I got to 'boot camp' the guys from Texas were being called 'TEX' and the one from Brooklyn was 'Brooklyn'. Well, I'm from LOUISIANA and I'll be damned if I was going to let them call me **LOUISE!**—I opted for the 'LOUIE' handle."

"Sorry I asked. I <u>knew </u>there'd be some crazy-assed explanation." Seth said, "Where do you come up with these weird tales, anyway?"

"'S the truth!"

"Roger, I think the afternoon helo launch would be a good place to start our coverage, Gilmore advised, "The helo lift-off is scheduled for 1300 (1:PM) so we'll meet on the flight deck right after noon chow."

"Aye, Aye, Chief."

"Then later the ship will be conducting night flight ops. That'll be another great opportunity for some really impressive shots. Just after sun down will give us just enough light to provide some detail on deck—then the afterburners of the jets will put the SPARK into the scenes."

"Sounds terrific to me, Chief." Roger replied.

"Tomorrow morning, the hi-lining operation will be another event that we'll need to cover. I'll work from the elevator level and you get high angles from the flight deck, both forward and aft of the 'island' (ship's command superstructure)," the Chief further instructed Roger.

"I think we're off to the races, Chief," Roger laughed.

"Yeah. Let's just pray the guys on the other ships, carry out their assignments as well."

The next two days were filled with gathering pix and interviews with crew members from the Pilot House OOD (Officer of the Deck) and Quarter Master at the wheel to the Chief Mess Manager and Airman

Recruit on 'Mess Cook' (KP) duty in the scullery. By the time they had covered all this, they were close to exhausting their film supply.

"Lt. Butterfield," the Chief inquired, "Can we arrange to pick up the other photogs in the morning? I think we've done about all the damage we can,—besides were down to the last three hundred feet of film, which I'd like to reserve for shots of our departure from the ship."

"I'll see what we can do about getting your team back to dry land. From what I've seen of your activities on board, I feel you did a pretty thorough job. We can sure use some media attention and we appreciate you guys' providing us with the ammo to do just that."

"Speaking for myself," Roger spoke up, "I thoroully enjoyed my stay on 'Tico'. I was just learning my way around this 'floating city'. I don't think I've ever lost my way so many times in such a confined space! I asked for directions so many times, crewmen were stopping to show me the way, even when I knew where I was headed!."

"It's one of the greater problems we have with new crewmen coming aboard," the Lt. laughed, "I guess we should issue a road map to everyone stepping off the gangplank."

"Wouldn' hurt, Sir."

Getting Seth and Baldy back aboard 'Tico' by helo was no problem, but the operation of another hi-line from the AKA Supply ship to bring Louie back, was deemed to be too complicated because of the ship's commitments to supplying other ships in the teak force.

So the decision was made to let Louie ride the AKA a couple more days until it's scheduled stop In Saigon where it was due to off-load some heavy equipment.

The Chief, Seth, Roger and Baldy gathered all their film and data reports and got them off on the afternoon courier flight on it's way to Washington. This accomplished, they loaded onto the COD for the flight back to Tan Son Nhut.

The launch from the flight deck was almost as exciting as their landing had been. Chief Gilmore warned the men that the 'kick' from the catapult-assisted take-off was a reverse of their landing jolt—

"You'll feel more like getting kicked in the butt by a Missouri Mule, when that thing 'sling-shots' you into the wild blue yonder," he informed them.

Later, Baldy reaffirmed the sensation.

"I'm going to have to see a chiropractor about putting my ass back on the right end of my spine, after that wild ride!" was his graphic description.

For the next couple days all was quiet at the 'House of the Rising Sun', as Team ALPHA One's 'Mad Man' Madison had christened their Saigon Villa.

That all came to a screeching halt, however, with the docking of the AKA and Louie's return from his adventure on the South China Sea.

Louie immediately began regaling the photographers with his many tales of his five-day tour as a 'sea-going' swabbie. This had been Louie's first encounter with the rocking and rolling of shipboard life and, for the first 24 hours, he spent most of his time hanging over the rail or the rim of the toilet hollering for 'O'ROURKE'.

His second day he recovered and proceeded to film everything that went on aboard the ship.

"Guys, you wouldn't believe all the stuff they carried in the holds of that tub. Everything from paper-clips to toilet paper. They moved cases and cases of canned fruit and vegetables, if Safeway stocks it, this ship carried twice as much," Louie told the men.

"We pulled along side three-to-five ships a day and hi-lined over to them cargo-net after cargo-net loaded with supplies. These guys worked from dawn to sometimes way after dark humping that stuff around." Louie marveled, "I burned a lot of film and I sure hope I did these men justice, their deeds have gone unsung for too long."

It took a couple days before Louie ran out of steam and fell silent. No one made light of Louie's sea-sick episode because most of them had suffered he same thing sometime in their Navy careers.

"I had a brief few moments of queasyness myself," Seth admitted, "When the helo first set me down on the deck of that Destroyer, it was bouncing around like a cork in a bathtub. I landed on my butt when I jumped out of the helo's hatch just as the ship came down off a swell and left me five feet in the air. My cheeks are still black-and-blue."

"I can sympathize with you there, Buddy," added Roger, "During my brief sea tour our ship crossed 'the line' (equator) and I had go through the 'Shell-back' initiation and my butt came out of that looking like a Concord Grape. Those crewmembers who had made a previous crossing into the realm of 'King Neptune' formed a gauntlet line which we 'pollywogs' (initiates) were forced to crawl through while they proceeded to pound our asses with three-foot sections of fire hose they had soaked in sea water and let dry in the sun. Some of those guys were really sadistic about it."

"What's 'sadistic'?" Baldy asked;

"Beats me," laughed Seth.

Baldy was puzzled by all the laughter that followed Seth's remark. 'What's so damn funny?'

"Baldy, if you want to know, look it up in the dictionary, otherwise you'll just have to SUFFER through it—which prompted additional hilarity from the team.

As a result of the bombing attack on the Army CID Villa during the team's last down-time, Lt. Crocket decided they needed some kind of security to ward off being the next targets.

"I think, Chief, we need to set up a dusk-to-dawn watch. I'll leave it up to you to come up with a plan."

"Aye, Aye, Sir." Gilmore turned to the assembled men, "Guys, I'm thinking we stand two-hour rotating watches. That'll allow everyone a longer uninterrupted sleep-time and no one should conk out on watch. Cox, since you have your finger on the roster, how about typing up the watch—list. Put everyone on it excluding the Lt.—"

"HOLD ON THERE, CHIEF—! I'LL BE TAKING MY TURN ALONG WITH THE REST OF YOU MUGS!" Lt Crocket interrupted, "This is a team operation and I'M A PART OF THIS TEAM!"

"Sorry, Lt., No disrespect intended. You got that Cox? IT'S ALL HANDS !."

As the sun went down, Chief Gilmore took his weapon and positioned himself on the balcony overlooking the street. Ten-to-a-dozen sandbags had been piled along the railing for cover and a couple more were piled to make a chair-like spot for the watch-stander's butt comfort.

"Lt., I think this is going to be a 'numba-one' O.P. (Observation Post)."

"Well, don't get too comfortable, Chief. Keep you eyes peeled and ears tuned. These bastards are sneaky."

"Don't sweat me, Lt., I'm just looking for an excuse to 'dust' a few more Commies!"

The night went undisturbed, much to Gilmore's disappointment.

"All's well this time," the Chief remarked, "I'm glad we all 'bit the bullet' but the Commies best not try us—we're ready and waiting for 'em."

The next night was proving to be as quiet as the first, until, at 0400 (4 AM) when Chief Gilmore went to relieve the watch and found Louie with his eyes tightly closed.

"***WAKE UP ! YOU GOLDBRICK !***" the Chief bellowed, waking the whole Villa populace. "You are on report for sleeping on watch !"

"But, Chief, I wasn't sleepin'. I only closed my eyes for a second to inspect my eyelids for light leaks," Louie pleaded.

"Don't give me that old sh—t, Sonny-boy. I heard that one when I was a 'boot' back in '42!!"

"Chief," the Lt. spoke up, "I think I have the appropriate punishment that'll just fit the situation. I was waiting 'til morning to tell you guys but COMNAVFORV (Commander Naval Forces Vietnam) has a C-45 Beech flying over to Bangkok Thursday and they invited us to send three deserving men along for a four-day R&R.

"Y'all will have to cut cards for which three get to go. But, Louie, for your little 'eyelid inspection' fiasco, you are eliminated from the drawing and will, instead, spend the four days 'field-daying' (extreme cleaning) the Villa and Office. Sound fair to the rest of you men?"

"**PERFECT, SIR !**" Was the unanimous reply.

After three nights of high alert security watches with no incidents, the Lt. announced:

"I've also decided the 'security watch' you've been standing is a waste of time. We ALL just have to keep alert and sleep with one eye open. The Com Sat (local cops) have stepped up their patrols of this sector so things are expected to calm down around here."

"That suits us fine, Lt.," said Gilmore, "I've been afraid one of these yard birds were liable to get excited and shoot one of us!"

Baldy, Seth and Roger were the winners of the high-card draw for the Thailand R & R trip. However, Roger decided he'd rather spend those four days at the Saigon USO with his fiancé, Xuan (Anne). Chief Gilmore, Cox and the Lt. proceeded to draw once more to fill third seat. Gilmore picked the high card so the passenger manifest was firm.

"Just a few words of warning for you three. Stay out of trouble while you're in Bangkok. The Status of Forces Agreement we have with Thailand can't offer you much legal protection in any civil action," Lt Crocket advised them, "They just assume you're guilty until you prove your innocence. Also, just DANCE with the dance-hall girls. Prostitution is rampant and SO ARE THE DESEASES that go with it !! Don't mess up your life for a brief 'fling'. Some of the 'bugs' being passed around don't yet have a cure.

"Put your time and talent to good use over there. Take your cameras along and try to pick up some good 'stock' footage of the people and places—Washington loves that kind of fluff."

"Most of all," the Lieutenant added, "Enjoy yourselves and COME BACK SAFE !"

The COMNAVFORV people had business so, on landing, the LCDR advised Gilmore and his cohorts they would be on their own until 0700 Monday morning.

"I've found, the best way to really see Bangkok," he told the men, "is to find a cabby and hire him for all four days to take you around. He' should only charge you $15 to $20 a day and they're all pretty dependable. It'll sure conserve you liberty-time by not having to walk or trying to hail a cab from place to place, and it's a sight cheaper."

"Thanks, Sir, we appreciate your help," replied the Chief.

It wasn't hard to find an available cab—they were bumper-to-bumper in front of the terminal, all making their 'pitch' for passengers.

"First thing we gotta do is find us a centrally locate hotel from where we can fan out over the rest of the city.," Gilmore suggested,

"Hey, driver, take us to a downtown hotel that ain't too high priced."

"Roger, wilco, Chief-son. Know just the place. It clean and good people."

"I'm about to starve," Baldy piped up. "As soon as we dump our junk let's find some good ole' Thai vittles."

"You got my vote, Baldy," Seth agreed.

"Know Numba One restaurant," their driver volunteered. "All G.I.s eat there. It got big steaks, cheeseburgers great food."

"Hell, I'm in Thailand. When I'm in a foreign country I always eat what the locals eat. I want some real <u>Thai grub,</u>"

"They got that, too. I eat there many time."

"OK, driver, that sounds great to us. By the way what do we call you besides 'driver'? the Chief asked.

"I called 'Bernie'. My Thai name too hard for G.I.s to say."

"Fine, 'Bernie', Let's chow down!"

Following a meal laced with curry and other weird spices, Bernie started their tour of Bangkok's scenery and attractions.

First stop was a personal tour of the famous 'River Market' where many exotic fruits and vegetables were peddled from native long-boats tied up along the docks and to each other.

Baldy bought a soccer-ball-size melon, and quickly sliced into it's bright red flesh. He bit into a big piece and, with red juice running down his chin like a school boy on a fourth of July picnic, exclaimed:

"HOLY JEHOSEPHAT ! THAT'S THE SWEETEST, JUICIEST MELON I <u>EVER</u> ATE !"

"Well, Baldy, I couldn't swear to the 'sweetest', but the <u>juiciest</u> IS OBVIOUS by the red river running down your hairy chin," the Chief guffawed.

"Have a taste, Chief. It's so sweet it's almost sickening."

Baldy proceeded to share his discovery with everyone including Bernie.

No one disagreed with Baldy's assessment.

"Sunday, before we leave I want to pick up a half-dozen of those beauties to take back to the Villa," Baldy promised. "Man, I'd like to take some seeds back to the states with me also, and set up my own little produce stand along a country road. My people all appreciate a good melon. They'll flip over these."

The men sampled a few other fruits available but none brought out the ravings produced by the melons. The rest of the day was spent visiting the Palace and the various Temples dotting Bangkok. Seth was taken by the beauty of the Buddhist Temples and their ornate gold covered religious statues and altars.

"Jeeze," Roger marveled on seeing all the gold and jewel-inlaid items filling the temples, "The major part of this countries wealth must be right here in plain sight."

"Well, Roger, don't get too excited—most of these things are only gold-leaf. A few smaller items might be solid gold, but the rest is just surface dressing," Said Seth, "In Harvard, before I 'got booted', I took a course in Far East Cultures, and learned a bit about this stuff."

"Well, it still makes my palms itch to see all that gold—leaf or solid," Roger replied.

The nightlife of Bangkok was also sampled and they all marveled at the ability of the Thai bands to imitate the styles of the 'Beatles', the 'Rolling Stones' and other American pop groups.

"If I didn't know better," Seth said, "I'd swear I was home spinnin' those records on my Hi-Fi !"

Baldy and Seth found partners and danced a few numbers, but Chief Gilmore begged off, saying:

"I never was much at dancin' and I never could get the hang of these new fangled moves."

A couple more club stops and the three agreed it was time to go back to the hotel for some of the 'relaxation' part of their trip.

The remainder of their 'R & R' involved more sight-seeing under guidance of Bernie and a final Saturday night 'on the town' for fine food and drink and a bit more dancing by Seth and Baldy.

Monday morning dawned on the exhausted trio of cameramen. Bernie picked them up and had them ready to board the C-47 at 0700 on the dot. The plane was barely airborne before the three were sawing logs.

ELEVEN

The team was all back together in the Villa. Louie had completed his penance and everyone was chomping at the bit to get on with the job.

They didn't have long to wait. Tuesday morning Lt. Crocket gathered the team in the office and started handing out assignments.

"Seth," he said, "I ran into a SeaBee PAO (Public Affairs Officer) at the 'O' Club last night, and he told me about a small detachment of CBs up in Hue, near the DMZ, who are involved in an effective 'People-to-People' program. He'd like to get some good PR stuff out of the story. I'm sending you on this one. You'll be on you own. I want a story-line with stills—and, if you can handle it—try for a few hundred feet of mopix."

"Aye, Aye, Sir !"

"Chief, I want you to take Louie and Roger on this next one. CINCPAC wants us to spend some time with the 'Riverine' boats patrolling the waterways down in the Mekong Delta. They've come under fire a few times so take flak-vests, helmets and weapons, just to cover your asses. You guys know what kinda' stuff CINCPAC likes so take along tak-son film. We make them happy, we stay happy."

"What ya' got for me?, Lt.," Baldy wanted to know, "I m 'R &R-ed' out and rarin' for some action before I start mildewin' in this hole someone called 'The Pearl of the Orient', I'm already beginin' to feel like an oyster !"

"Well, Baldy," the Lt. assured him, "I've been saving you 'til last. COMNAVFORV would like a bunch of footage of the city of Saigon.

I guess they're looking for sort of 'travelogue' type pictures. Never mind stills, just mopix. Give 'em lots of street stuff, markets, buildings and especially people. Nobody in the 'states' can even <u>imagine</u> the wild traffic, so shoot lots of that. That's something that is beyond description. 'Pictures are worth a thousand words'."

"I can handle that, Lt., I'm gonna' rent me a Vespa™ and sashay all over Saigon with my camera rollin'."

"OK, Son, but don't get yourself killed on one of those things. If you do, you know, we'll have to count you AWOL at morning muster."

"That's interesting to know, Sir. I hope I don't disappoint you but I plan to keep this torso scratch-free!"

Seth found the only C-130 flight going north for the next 48 hours could only take him as far as Da Nang. From there he would have to hoof-it the 60 ± miles to Hue or hitch a ride on whatever vehicle he could hook up with.

On the advise of the Air Force Sgt. at the Da Nang check-in desk, he ambled over to the Marine Supply Depot warehouse and discovered they had a two-truck convoy headed his way in a couple of hours.

"You got time to hit the NCO Club for some chow, if you want," the Marine Corporal advised, "I'll send someone for you when we're ready to roll."

"Thanks, Corporal. I appreciate that."

As promised, a Vietnamese found Seth at the Club and informed him:

"Trucks all loaded. Di-di soon. Corporal say grab junk and hop on!"

Two 3-ton trucks were just finishing gassing up when Seth arrived ready to shove off.

Riding the roads of Vietnam was not the most comfortable or safest mode of getting from one place to another. The highways were often mined or the trucks were ambushed. Seth's luck held and they arrived in Hue without incident.

"Thanks, Guys. If you know where we can get some 'cool ones' I'll buy a round—OR TWO!"

Of course, being Marines, they were well aware of the location of the nearest watering-hole and Seth and the Marines relaxed over a couple of Bah-Me-Bahs (Vietnamese #33 beers), before tackling the job of unloading their cargo.

After more 'Thanks', Seth grabbed his camera gear and went looking for the CB group whose story he was assigned to report.

Hue had once been the capitol of Vietnam but due to the exodus of war refugees the population had dwindled to a few thousand. Parts of the city were like a ghost-town. Buildings were damaged by frequent shelling from the North. Being within 'spittin' distance of the DMZ made the city the frequent target of the Communist forces.

A few questions and Seth was soon directed to the hooch where the CBs resided.

"Welcome to our 'digs'," The First Class Petty Officer in charge, greeted him.

"I'm Builder First Class Billy Matlock. Everybody just calls me 'Mat'. We got the word that you're going to spend a few days with us to make us celebrities. We'd just as soon remain 'incognito' but our CO says he wants to 'toot our horn'. So, who are we to argue with a Lieutenant Commander?"

"I'll try not to disrupt your operation while I'm here. I will need to do some interviewing to get the info I'll need for the story, and I also will have to have access to any of your work which might provide picture ops," Seth told them.

"No problemo, Partner. Our operation, as you call it, is to help the people here in any way we can. We work with USAID (US Aid for International Development) and a couple Catholic Nuns.

"We're doing some reconstruction work on the local orphanage that the Nuns run and we're trying to do something about getting clean drinking water to the people. Only about one-fourth of the city has unpolluted water. Typhus and other water-born diseases are rampant," Mat informed Seth.

"Sounds to me like there's more than one story to tell here," Seth replied, "I'm anxious to get started."

"OK Seth' We'll be heading out on our orphanage project first thing in the morning. You get your camera and pencils ready and we'll roll at 0800!"

"I'll be rarin' to go. I've got lots of good ideas to work on."

The CBs laid on a hearty breakfast and, true to Mat's prediction, by 0800, they were aboard their two trucks, loaded with tools and materials, and headed for the orphanage.

Seth was busy filming every move the CBs made—their hands, the intenseness of their faces, their sweat-covered muscles—documenting every phase of their reconstruction of the run-down buildings.

"Boy, the weather's perfect, the light is right. This is going to be one scrumptious hunk of film.!" Seth exclaimed., "CHINFO (Chief of Navy Information) is going to cream their jeans over this report, you betchum!"

Seth was able to get his close-ups, his medium shots and establishing (long) scenes, and everything was coming together with the perfection of a 'Hollywierd' epic.

It was fortunate that Seth was able to get so much coverage on that first day, because, on the second day, the dark clouds rolled in and the monsoon rains washed out any hopes of getting any external shots.

Seth, however, showed his ingenuity and foresight by packing two Frezzo™ battery-powered lights. These were quickly put into play, and Seth continued to film while the CBs worked on the interior of the structure

"All is not lost," he commented to Mat "If life hands you lemons— make lemonade—and look for someone life has handed VODKA!"

"Man, Seth, you got a screwball answer for everything, haven't you?" Mat chuckled.

"Well, if you're already nuts you have to fight to keep from going insane!" Seth retorted.

"I'm not so sure some of us haven't already crossed that line, Partner!"

"Mat, it's a BIG CLUB and there's always room for one more. I have about five-weeks to go on my tour and I'm fighting to go back sound in body AND MIND !"

The day passed with no problems for Seth OR the CB workers.

Day three was highlighted by one of the CBs showing up with a beat-up old peddle-powered sewing machine.

"It's going to need some fixin' but I think, with a little welding and pounding, I can make it operational for the nuns," the CB said, "They've been hand-stitching to make clothes for these kids long enough.

"When I found this thing in the ruins of a building west of town, I saw right away a use for it at the orphanage."

"You did good O'Malley. That's the ol' CB 'CAN DO' SPIRIT! You concentrate on getting that thing functioning. When you're finished we'll make a presentation of it to Sister Margaret and Sister Marie. We'll make a real CB party of it—and Seth can photograph it for our CO, he'll bust his buttons showing it to the other COs !"

"CHINFO will be pretty pleased, too," Seth agreed, "They eat this kinda' stuff up back in DC."

O'Mallley spent a day and a half cobbling up repairs on the machine and, when he had finished with the job, demonstrated by sewing a SeaBee patch on his fatigue blouse.

"That sure does the trick," he reported, "Those nuns can really run off some fine 'duds' for the kids now."

"O'Malley, you never cease to amaze me with all your talents. Now you're a sewing machine mechanic," Mat marveled.

"Hell, Mat, my old man used to preach that you can do anything you really put your mind to, and I say—'cain't never did nothing'."

"Now, to plan the surprise party for the Sisters." Mat said.

The eight men whipped up a fine 'spread' with Seth photographing every step. A few colorful ribbons hanging from the bare rafters dressed up the classroom and the invite went out to the nuns and orphans to come join the party.

The Sisters were dumbfounded when O'Malley rolled in the refurbished tailoring instrument.

The Party was a rip-roaring success and, needless to say, everyone was happy with the results. Even Seth was overwhelmed with the photo opportunities he was afforded by the festivities.

Setting aside the work on the orphanage, the CBs moved over to their other priority project—installing a filtering and purification system in the city's only remaining operative well. The machinery and equipment had been the major part of the cargo brought in by the Marine trucks that had transported Seth to Hue.

Getting everything set up and installed was a back-braking and lengthy piece of work but, true to CB tradition, they completed it in three days. It was now ready to run tests. For this they brought in a USAID Environmental Health doctor. A few minor adjustments and the city's meager water source was declared 'SAFE'. To further prove it's quality to the citizenry the whole CB team drank a toast to the completion of another CB 'CAN DO' PROJECT.

Following the wrapping-up of the water supply job, Seth sat down and typed up his stories and data sheets and prepared to return to Da Nang with the Marine trucks that had brought him to Hue a week ago.

"You guys are doing a bang-up job here and I just hope my stuff will do it justice," he told Mat and his men, "I'll leave you with a wish for Good Luck, and I hope I see you in 'the GOOD OLD US of A' sometime !"

Chief Gilmore, Louie and Roger had joined up with 'Riverine' PBRs (fast river patrol boats) and, at the very outset, were experiencing a wild adventure. They were not being fired on but the sailor at the helm had the boat flying up the Mekong River at warp speed, was zigging and zagging from side to side.

"We don't dare go in a straight line for fear of making us 'sittin' ducks' for any 'Charlie' lurking in the riverbank brush," the First Class Bos'n at the helm explained to the Chief, "We're just here to prevent the Commies from using these rivers to run guns and supplies to their Delta outposts. We 'engage' them only if we're fired on. Much of the river traffic is legit. We stop any suspicious boats and inspect them for contraband. If we find any we take their boat in tow back to our base."

"I understand the evasive maneuvering," Gilmore replied, "But it's mighty hard to get any steady mopix when we could tumble over the side if we don't hang on for dear-life."

"That's why every seat has a harness to keep your butts anchored to the boat. Be sure you buckle up snug. If we have to turn around to pick up any 'drift-wood' we do it at high speed and it's a rough landing when we jerk you back aboard !"

"Hey, Gunner," Louie asked the man on the forward 70 caliber gun mount, "Ain't you scared of fallin' overboard on theses snap turns?"

"Not as long as I have my harness snapped on to anchor me down!"

"Yeah, but what if you didn't have that harness?"

"Then I'd be 'scared of falling overboard' !"

"That answer your asinine question, Louie.? You ask a stupid question you get a stupid answer!" Gilmore laughed.

As the PBR roared up the river no other craft were encountered but everyone still maintained a sharp lookout for any movement on the water or in the brush along the river banks.

About an hour into their run, the gunner on the bow shouted over the roar of the engines—

"Hey, Boats' I just saw a dugout with three men on board, ziggy into that small stream on the starboard. They headed into some of that overhanging brush on the south side."

"Hang on Guys, we're coming about. We'll cruise in there and check them out," the bos'n at the wheel warned.

"Be alert, Men. If they're VC we might have a fight on our hands. But hold your fire until I give the signal. We don't want to 'snuff' some friendly taking his crop to market."

The three Vietnamese were flushed out of the jungle and, with the help of the PBR's interpreter who rides along on these missions, determined that all they had were three very terrified farmers heading for Vung Tao with rice and produce. They were immediately released and left to wash out their soiled scivies.

"Back to square one," the Bos'n in charge of the PBR said.

"I got some really good stuff of our little encounter," Roger told the Chief;

"So did I," Louie added, "I got some fine close-ups of their faces during the questioning. I want to get some facials of the interpreter, too, now that were out of the woods"

"That's the way to work it, Guys, Between what you shot and my stuff we have a great start on this project;" said Gilmore.

No more small boats were sighted and the PBR was turned around headed back to base. About an hour's ride down the Mekong they started taking small-arms fire from the brush on the port side.

"Hang on men, we got trouble! I'm going to have to take some evasive action in order to get into position to pour some lead their way. <u>Get that forward 70 blazing,</u> Gunny. Spray the brush like you're watering the flowers.

"You men aft, brake out those two RPGs (rocket propelled grenade launchers) and blow some holes in those 'Dinks'

The jungle along the river became a Fourth of July fireworks display when all the PBR's weapons were brought into play. A half hour into the action the VC must have decided they'd knocked over a bees' nest and they di-di-ed for far away places.

"Everybody OK ?" the Bos'n shouted.

"The gangs all here and in one piece." the aft gunners reported.

"All 's well in the forward post," the bow-gunner added.

"I could use three or four more of those 70 calibers and maybe another couple RPGs. They really reduced the VC's desire to stick around when my guys opened up on them," said the Bos'n, with a slight chuckle.

"Boats, I don't blame them for losing their enthusiasm for the fight. No one in their right mind would stay to face all that fire-power," Chief Gilmore agreed.

"OK. Let's head this baby for home and hope we don't run into any more of those 'slope-heads' before we tie up."

"I hardly had time to put my eye to my viewfinder before it was all over," Louie complained.

"I was fiddling around with my Arriflex™ when they hit us. So I was all set and fired it up in time to get several feet of the whole shebang," Roger bragged, "I forgot all about my weapon, but I guess we had enough sh—t flying their way without it. Jeeze, it sounded like all hell had broke loose when those RPGs and that 70 cranked up. I think those 'dinks' had visions of hell descending on them!"

"I managed to only get off a couple of minutes coverage before they 'bugged-out', too," the Chief added, "That was short and sweet. Especially if we snuffed some of them little bastards."

It took another hour-and-a-half of zig-zagging down the river before they reached the moderate safety of their base in Vung Tao.

They learned on their arrival at the PBR base that there was only one scheduled flight for Tan Son Nhut that evening. The Canadian Air Force had a 'Canberra' turbo-prop taking off at dusk and Chief Gilmore finagled a ride for the crew of weary cameramen.

The aircraft was not rigged for passengers so the men had to sit on the cargo and 'jury-rig' straps to use as 'seat' belts.

It was lucky that the Canadian cargo-master made the 'seat-belt' suggestion because, as the plane began it's descent for landing, tracer bullets started whizzing by on both sides of the aircraft.

The pilot immediately began a full-power climb and bank to get out of the shooters' range.

"HANG ON, LADS !" the cargo-master shouted. Which really wasn't necessary as all of the photographers were gripping anything in sight to hold them from going airborne.

"This is going to be a 'hairy' landing, Yanks, so brace yourselves," the pilot announced, *"I'm going to have to come over the field high to avoid the bullets, and make a steep dive hoping I can pull this baby up as we reach the runway—it's what we flyboys call a 'CONTROLLED CRASH' ! HERE WE GO-O-O-O.*

Seconds later the Canberra made contact with the ground, bounced a couple times and settled down to taxi to the hangar.

"HOLY SH-—T!" Louie exclaimed, "I've ridden about every roller-coaster in the south and ain't none can hold a candle to that ride! It'll be a week before my ass un-puckers!"

"Just thank GOD we can walk away from that one," Gilmore commented, "They say 'any crash you can walk away from is a good landing'—now I believe it!"

"Let's get our gear stowed in the office and ziggy over to the NCO Club. I need a half dozen 'Buds' to get me settled down," Gilmore added.

Seth had returned from Hue and Baldy had turned in his scooter and both were already camped out in the Club having dinner and drinks when Gilmore and his crew walked in.

"Hail, Hail, the 'Gangs' all here," yelled Baldy, "Have a seat, Guys, and let's get down to some serious drinking. I know we all could suffer through a few dozen 'Buds'."

"The tenth round is on me," Louie volunteered, "Chief, call Lt. Crocket and tell him he might as well join us, 'cuz that's the only way he's going to get to see us before noon tomorrow,. I'm 'homesteading' a table closest to the bar and I ain't movin' fer nobody!"

True to their word, they 'camped out' in the Club until the two o'clock closing, then purchased five cases of ice-cold 'Bud' and adjourned to the Office where they 'partied-out' for a couple more hours—until one by one they zonked out.

That's where the Lt. found them in the morning—all crapped out and splayed over chairs and desks "like bodies in a morgue" as he later described it to the survivors.

"COME BACK TO THE LAND OF THE LIVING, YOU SOTS," Lt. Crocket yelled, "We could be getting new assignments any minute and I want a sharp, sober team ready to roll. Soak your heads in some cold water and have a pint of coffee. R & Rs' over."

"DAMN, Lt., I wish you'd lower your voice," Louie complained, "You're taking the top of my head off if you speak above a whisper."

"Too bad, Louie, but what are you going to do if you go out on patrol today and some 'dink' pops a grenade in your vicinity? You'd best down a couple aspirins and get yourself straight."

The team 'lucked out' this day as no word came down from 7th Fleet or CINCPAC of any new operations upcoming for at least 48 hours. Rest and QUIET soon had most of the men back to near-normal physical and neurological shape.

"I'm starving," Baldy announced, "Anyone for a walk over to the Victory for some vittles?"

The entire team was of the same mind so they trooped over to their favorite Chinese restaurant to put some lining back into their suffering stomachs.

The balance of the day Chief Gilmore had everyone stripping down their cameras and weapons for a complete cleaning and refurbishing.

"This humidity and the jungle dust and sand can stop your equipment from functioning at the most inconvenient time. 'Cleanliness is next to—SURVIVAL'—to paraphrase what my Mama used to preach," the Chief admonished the men.

"Would you listen to the 'old philosopher'," Seth laughed.

"Laugh, if you like, Guys, but I'm going to hold inspection on your gear when we're through and WOE! to the f—ck-up I find with a spot of grime or dirt on his tools!"

"I'll second the Chief's warning," added the Lt., "We can't take on any undue risk of equipment or personal failure! None of **my** team is going to be shipped home in a body-bag or on a stretcher!"

"AHMEN," responded everyone.

TWELVE

American forces in Vietnam were building rapidly and to keep up with the growth, more and more bases are being established. Newest and largest of these is a giant port with fuel and ammunition depots to support the troops

"Vietnam is becoming so crowded with 'round eyes', "Roger commented, "that it's getting 'disoriented'."

"'PUN' or not, Roger, there's a lot of truth in what you say," Lt. Crocket answered, "That new port being built in Cam Ranh Bay is our next priority, Guys. COMNAVFORV wants us to spend a week or so documenting the progress.

"The majority of the work is being done by MPR, a civilian contractor, however, the Seabees are pouring in a couple battalions to handle a huge portion of the personnel facilities. Our whole team will be involved in this one so be prepared to spend some time and a whole lot of effort on it. This is HUGE, and our ass is on the block to put forth our max coverage!"

Helo transport was not available due to other commitments so Lt. Crocket decided to utilize the van and drive the 70 to 80 miles.

"There's not much in the way of highways between Saigon and Cam Ranh Bay," the Lt. said, "but COMUSMACV Operations has provided me with a fairly recent map of the route."

The team spent the following day rounding up and packing the camera gear and personal-needs for the extended stay away from the Villa.

"I sure hope they thought to start by building a mess hall AND CLUB," was Baldy's main concern, "Nights get mighty long if there's no provision for relaxing at the end of a hard day's work."

"Food and drink is all you think about, eh, Baldy?"

"Oh, I think about other things, too, but those other 'things' can get me in trouble."

"Baldy, you're going to be the chauffeur so run the van over to the motor pool and have it checked out bumper to bumper," the Lt. ordered, "And this time **DON'T FORGET TO TOP OFF THE GAS TANK!,** We don't need to get stranded half way to Cam Rahn Bay like the last time you got us marooned on a detour around Saigon. We just might not be lucky enough this time to find a boy with a water buffalo to tow us to a gas station in exchange for a couple of candy bars!"

Seth was assigned to ride the 'shotgun' seat and navigate for Baldy. So he immediately set about studying the map.

"We're depending on you to navigate and keep the 'Hairy-one' from getting us lost or stranded in the 'boon docks'!"

"Aye, Aye, Sir."

"I'm going to ride along on this one, also, just to 'grease' the skids with the brass and make sure they know what your primary and **only** job is. But I have work at the office that needs my attention so I'll only stay a couple days."

"It's good to have the whole team together in the field, Lt. Glad to have you along." the Chief replied.

Early in the morning the little caravan got under way and things were going along according to plan—until, two hours after their start, Seth announced:

"Lt., This numbskull has got us lost already! I told him to turn <u>*right*</u> *a mile or so back, and he must have turned* <u>*LEFT*</u> *! I took my eyes off the road to check the map and that was just long enough for Hair Brain here to f—ck up! We got to turn around and back-track to the last intersection in order to get back on course!"*

"Baldy, pay attention!" Lt. Crocket yelled, "We don't have time for you to fart around! That's why I handed Seth the map and figured, between the two of you, we'd cruise along without a screw-up.! Maybe Roger ought to take the wheel"

"I'm sorry Sir. It won't happen again, I guaranty it!"

"It better NOT!"

After getting back on track, the trip proceeded without further problems and, just before sun down, Baldy guided the van through the base security gate.

"Now, to find the CB HQ and coordinate our operation," Lt Crocket said, "We have to find berthing. I want you men humpin' it at first light."

They flagged down an MP patrolling the base and obtained directions to the CB Operations tent. There the LCDR (Lieutenant Commander) in charge directed the duty Yeoman to assign the enlisted men to bunks in the CB barracks, and he escorted Lt. Crocket to the Officers' Quarters.

"Our accommodations here aren't the 'Beverly Hilton', but it's home sweet home," the LCDR informed Lt. Crocket, "By the way, my name is Mallory, Andrew Mallory. We don't stand too much on formality so just call me 'Andy'."

"Fine. And you can call me 'Crocket',—or whatever else comes to mind. Just don't let me miss chow or payday," the Lt. chuckled.

Construction activities were well under way when the photo team finished breakfast and sat for a quick safety briefing. They were anxious to get started and eagerly scattered to pick the area of their coverage. Seth started by getting interviews and photos for release to the Seabees' home media, Louie opted to film the carpenters and welders assembling the warehouses and other buildings that were to house the HQ, a sick bay and permanent barracks for the personnel. Roger and Baldy finagled a jeep and were following the heavy equipment operations.

The Chief occupied his time shooting long-shots and location views that would tie everything together when it came to editing their film back in DC.

"Hey, Baldy," Roger suggested, "Why don't we go over there where the huge earth-movers are scooping up the earth? That ought to give us some impressive shots."

"OK, Hang on. There ain't no roads to follow. We just have to hop from one mound of sand to the next, but we'll get there—right side up, I HOPE!"

Baldy had the jeep leaping from one pile to the next like a 'motor-cross' racer, jarring their tails with every landing.

"What's the hurry, you crazy nut?" Roger sceamed, "They'll still be there twenty minutes from now!"

"Roger, this is a kick. Hang on and enjoy the ride. Coney Island was never this much fun!"

"But Coney Island's rides ended safe and sound. I'm not too sure this ride has any such guaranty!"

To Roger's extreme relief, Baldy pulled up near the earth-moving giants and brought his camera to bear and began recording the action.

"Roger, stay with the jeep. I'm going to see if the driver will let me aboard to I get some coverage from another angle."

With some crazy hand signals, Baldy was able to get his request across and the driver pulled up and signed for Baldy to climb up beside him.

Baldy was having a ball riding the big machine and photographing the driver's hands on the controls and his expressions of concentration. Fifteen minutes of that and Baldy figured he had enough, so the driver stopped to let him off.

Just as Baldy was stepping away from the earthmover a bull-dozer came charging by and had to take a sudden turn to avoid running over Baldy. The 'dozer' took a nose-dive into a ditch and the civilian contract driver had to jump to save his own skin.

"YOU DUMB, HAIRY ASSED CHIMPANZEE!!" he screamed at Baldy, *"YOU BETTER WATCH OUT OR I'LL PLOW YOU UNDER THIS AIRSTRIP!"*

"Sorry 'bout that!—**And I ain't no chimpanzee**—I'm more like a **GORILLA** which I'll demonstrate for you, if you come over here, YOU RED-HEADED 'PECKER-HEAD'!"

"Ease off, Baldy!" Roger warned, "We don't need no incident here, today! Get back in the jeep and let's di-di!"

Baldy was still shaking and itching to tangle with the red-headed bull-dozer driver, but Roger's cool head prevailed and he climbed back into the Jeep and Roger took the wheel to get them far away from the scene.

A couple more hours of filming (in a new location) and Roger and Baldy pulled up to the mess hall just in time for noon chow call.

The rest of the team joined them and Roger proceeded to relate the story of Baldy's encounter with the MPR diver.

"Yeah. He was charging around on that bull-dozer like he was on the streets of Saigon," Baldy added, "He deserved to wind up in the ditch! Maybe it'll slow him down."

"Just be glad he didn't slice and dice you with that 'dozer," the Chief admonished him.

Seth reported that he had full cooperation from the Seabee personnel and bragged about the numerous home-town stories he was able to produce in one morning's work.

"I think CHINFO (Chief of Navy Information) will have a field day with all the releases they'll get out of this stuff."

"Louie, How'd you make out on your project?" Lt. Crocket asked.

"Couldn't have been better, Sir. These Seabees are a great bunch. They made me feel just like one of their's. They even invited me to have a few 'cool ones' with them at the Club tonight."

"Well, let's just hope this afternoon goes as smooth as this morning—with exception taken in the Baldy vs. 'Peckerhead' case—," Chief Gilmore offered, "Now, will someone please pass me another piece of that apple pie?"

Later that afternoon Lt. Crocket informed Louie:

"Louie, I have you set up for an hour of Helo time in the morning to get some aerials of the area. You be ready right after first light. The low angle of the sun in the morning will throw some shadows and give better definition to the buildings and working equipment. Later in the day with the sun more overhead everything is pretty flat-lighted and blends together too much."

"That's great, Sir. I need to get some more time in the air this month, anyway, to qualify for my Hazardous Flight Pay."

"Yeah," Seth remarked, "We are all a little short of hours right now and it's getting close to the end of the month."

"We'll be back in Tan Son Nhut shortly and you can book your necessary hops to qualify, then," the Lt. assured the men.

Louie and his cameras were airborne right after morning chow and was parked on an in-board seat as they started their first pass over the construction site.

"You'll have a better view if you come over here in the hatch," the Airman advised him, "Just hook yourself up to this gunner's belt and step out on the wheel-strut. That way you don't get the aircraft in your shot."

"I don't know about that, fella." Louie said in a shaky voice.

"What's the matter? You 'fraid of falling?"

"It's not the 'fallin' that bothers me—it's the sudden stop at the bottom!"

"I've heard that from about every passenger we ever carried," the Airman laughed.

Louie proceeded to harness up and followed the Airman's instructions.

A couple of passes North to South and a couple more from East to West and Louie gave the signal to return to base.

As he disembarked he thanked the Pilot and crew for a very smooth flight.

"I got some great footage of the construction and the port and I sure appreciate the use of your 'bird'."

While Louie was making like his passes over the base, the rest of the cameramen were dispatched to the water front where a dredge and pile-drivers were preparing to start building a system of piers capable of docking four to six cargo ships. LCDR Mallory said the port would cut down on the shipping traffic on the Saigon River and speed up the turn-around time for the supply ships—plus avoid the mines the VC liked to plant on the River.

With the CCG photographers all covering different phases of the work, by afternoon they had pretty much saturated the pier operation and were ready to call it a day as the light faded.

LCDR Mallory informed the Lt. that the Seabees were planning a beach party that evening and the photo crew was invited.

"There's a great stretch of beach for R&R on the north side of the port project. My guys are going to cook up some hotdogs and hamburgers along with plenty of 'beverages'," he told them, "We can all use a break and I don't think your team will mind kickin' back, havin' a swim and downing some home-style grub."

"That's a foregone conclusion, without me even asking them," Lt. Crocket replied.

Lt. Crocket returned to Saigon on a Tan Son Nhut bound helo the next morning, leaving the crew to wrap up the project in the following two or three days.

About all that was left for them to complete was a few close-ups and a couple hours of live sound recording of the machines, the hammering and other work-related noises, that the editors back in DC could cut into the final documentary. They also needed to type up their data sheets and package up their exposed film and have it ready for quick shipment on the first courier flight to DC.

"We get that done, and we can 'Di-Di Mau' for home," the Chief told the men.

All tasks completed, their last evening was spent partying with the Seabees and a few MPR employees. One of those employees was the red-head 'dozer driver Baldy had had words with.

Baldy showed his metal, though and went over to the red-head's table. The driver stood up preparing to do battle, but Baldy held out his hand and offered him a beer.

"We're all on the same side over here," he said, "So there ain't much point in fighting each other, Lets save it for the 'dinks'."

"Right you are, Gorilla," agreed the worker to resounding applause from the crowd (which had been expecting a knock-down drag-out war).

Everyone in the Club raised their glasses and shouted—**HOORAH!**

When the gang was ready to leave, a vote was taken as to who was to do the driving on the return trip. By a narrow margin of four-to-one Seth was elected, thus over-riding Baldy's one dissenting objection.

"We want to get there **today**, Baldy. Not sometime next week!" Chief Gilmore told him, "You took leave of your sense of direction on the way over. We can't afford that on our return."

It was a 'breeze' getting back to Tan Son Nhut, with Seth guiding the van. They all breathed a sigh of relief as Seth engineered the vehicle through the security gates of the airfield.

"I never thought the sight of our Office would be so welcome, but I'm glad to be back," Louie remarked, "I just hope the Lt. hasn't lined up any more trips for a couple of days. I got to get 'Mama San' to wash out my fatigues before I head out, again."

"I think we all smell a little 'gamey' and could use some soap-and-water on our duds as well as ourselves," Roger added, "I want to get spiffed up and go see Anne. "I'm getting more and more anxious to rotate back to 'ConUS' so we can get hitched."

"Our tour should be finished in three or four weeks, and I think we're all getting a little 'Asiatic'," Seth observed.

THIRTEEN

Saigon was quiet and the photo team took advantage of the peaceful night to catch up on some long needed shut-eye.

Lots of bed-rest and a bit of shopping at the Cho Lon Base Exchange to stock up on deodorant (very necessary in 'Nam), shaving gear and toothpaste. Also hours of maintenance work on cameras and weapons to be ready for the next call.

A surprise awaited the photographers on their return to their Villa Monday night—someone had hurled a huge chunk of concrete through the front window on the second floor.

Tied to the missile was a crudely scribbled note—'**YANKEE GO HOME!**'

"Looks like someone doesn't like our company." Louie remarked, "Well, I'd di-di home in one shake of a squirrel's tail, if CINCPAC would just say the word!"

"Amen!" was the unanimous response.

There was no way of getting the window replaced until the next day. This made it necessary for the men to spray the house and sleep under mosquito-netting to keep from being eaten alive by the insects.

"I'll get onto Public Works first thing in the morning and have them fix that," the Lt. told the group, "We can't afford to have anyone coming down with malaria or any of the other quaint diseases Vietnam offers."

The call to action wasn't long in coming. The day after their visit by the VC or 'cowboy's' (Vietnam juvenile delinquents) welcoming visit, Lt. Crocket broke the news that another big 'push' was about to require there services. A brigade of Marines were going to be heading it up and CINCPAC wanted "complete coverage". This meant all five photojournalists would be involved.

"This one is likely to be a really 'hairy' one, so make sure all your 'survivor's paper-work' is in order. I pray none of you will need it, but fate has a 'fickle finger'," the Lt. warned the men,

"I'm told the Communists have two or three hundred ARVN and a few hundred more North Vietnamese Regulars dug in about thirty clicks (km) to the west of Da Nang. We need to turn 'em back or 'snuff' 'em before they can begin their move south.

"Keep your cameras rollin' but your helmets and vests on and your butts down!. I'll be in constant contact with the Marine office here at COMUSMACV (the Military Assistance Command) in order to follow the action. AND I'LL BE ROOTIN' FOR YOU the whole time.

"The jump-off will start from Red Beach in Da Nang two days from now. That means you have to hop a flight to Da Nang first thing in the morning. Get a good night's rest and no 'Clubbing' for anyone tonight. I want you all 'bright eyed and bushy tailed' for this party!"

Da Nang was getting more and more crowded because of the rapid personnel build-up and traffic had increased to about the same level as Saigon. The citizens were prospering on the 'Yankee Dollars' being poured into the economy. Everyone had motor scooters, mopeds or motorcycles and they all vied for the-right-of-way. Along with the increase in noise level also came clouds of carbon monoxide sufficient to suffocate a horse.

"This place has sure 'mushroomed' since the last time I was here," Seth commented, "It used to be a quaint little town—now look at it!"

"I can't say as I like what this 'war' has done for the new life-style," added Roger.

The plane bringing the team to Da Nang had barely stopped taxiing before a Marine half-ton pulled up alongside to pick up the photographers and their equipment.

The Marine driver wasted no time whisking the men off to the Marine Red Beach base. There they were met by the Marine Battalion Public Affairs Officer, Capt. Hugh Morgan.

"You men will bunk down for the night in Barracks Five and we'll be pulling out at 0900," he informed them, "I don't need to remind you, this is going to be a tough one so make like boy scouts and '**BE PREPARED**'! I've heard how you CCG guys like to joke and and clown around, but you best remember—your's and other's lives are on the line the next few days!"

"Sir," Chief Gilmore spoke up, "We know our light-hearted reputation, but when it comes down to our attitude under fire—we're **VERY SERIOUS** professionals, committed to doing our job and doing it WELL!"

"No offense intended, Chief, I only wanted to impress on you that we're going into a hornet's nest and I sure don't want any casualties due to any lax alertness."

"No 'offense' taken, Captain. I just wanted to **impress on you**, we're dedicated to getting our job accomplished and coming back with a whole skin. I don't want any casualties to my men **or** any of the Marines we'll be accompanying."

"Good, then we understand each other! Now—the NCO Club is open so let's all stop by there and have a drink to the success of our mission. I'll spring for the first round."

"Thanks, Captain. But, I'd suggest that we hold it down to two or three 'rounds' in view of tomorrow's little jungle jaunt," Gilmore answered.

"Right you are, Chief."

Reveille rousted the camp and preparations for the engagement were well under way by the time the photo team had put on their vests and strapped on their packs. The contents of their packs consisted of a couple changes of scivies and socks and Tak Son film. The under-garments were secondary, but they were carrying enough film to launch a Hollywood feature film!

"CINCPAC said they wanted 'major coverage', and by God we're going to give it to them," Chief Gilmore declared, "Anyone who comes back with less than 500 feet of action film didn't do his job!"

The caravan of tanks, armored personnel carriers and trucks carrying the Marine combat troops and the photographers, pulled out of Red Beach Base with the sun barely peaking over the surrounding mountain tops. The forward Marine outposts were only about an hour's drive and, on arriving, the troops deployed along a north-south line and took up positions awaiting the orders to **'Move up!'** The photo crew split up and each joined up with their assigned company.

Excitement of the moment at hand, was at stress-level and fingers were itching on the triggers and shutter-releases.

They didn't have long to wait until the word came down the line to **'MOVE OUT!'**

The cameras began rolling but no one fired their weapons until they reached the tree line. That's when all hell broke loose! The firing came first from the tree-tops where dozens of snipers had strapped themselves to the top-most branches and were trying to pick off the nearest Marines.

Two Marines went down near Roger and there followed a rattling fire of Marine AR-15s on full automatic spraying every tree and scattering branches and VC in all directions.

Roger was pinned down briefly, but, as the firing let up slightly, he managed to get his camera rolling and got excellent shots of the Marines firing and the VC tumbling out of the trees.

As the Marine lines slowly advanced further into the jungle, firing became more sporadic. Gilmore and Louie were treated to their share of enemy resistance and managed to photograph the action of the Marine riflemen engaging the enemy close up.

Because the VC were so concealed in the heavy under-brush both photographers were having to concentrate on filming the Marines reactions and their faces as they fought to destroy the enemy just as the enemy was trying to destroy them.

Seth and Baldy were at the far north end of the Marine lines and had not yet run into enemy fire. Fifteen minutes into their advance, though, they began to receive mortar rounds. As the VC began to 'walk' their firing closer and closer one fell within six yards of their position and the Marines on each side of Seth were hit by shrapnel.

Seth miraculously was unscathed but he would forever remember the sound of the fragments cutting down the brush all around him, missing his head by fractions of an inch.

"Guys, I mean to tell you, I could hear old Satan beckoning me," Seth later stated.

Baldy, who was a couple hundred yards away, heard the exploding mortar shells but was soon distracted by a fusillade of rifle and machinegun fire in front of his own position. The enemy was well hidden in the jungle under-brush so Baldy was also limited to filming the Marine side of the battle. In spite of having good cover, bullets were buzzing like hornets all around him. One round hit Baldy in his vest and knocked the wind out of him, another ricocheted off the top of his helmet.

With all the CCG team it was as if their Guardian Angels were working overtime. As the day began to fade the word ws passed down:

"Hold your ground. Advance no further. Keep a sharp lookout for crawling two-legged snakes, they like to strike in the darkness!"

Everyone hunkered down and, with an alert lookout posted, attempted to grab a few winks before dawn introduced more fighting.

Seth's group was attacked during the night but vigilance paid off and the attackers were met with a withering outburst of machinegun fire and grenades which quickly discouraged the enemy from any further attempts to take out this Marine position.

The sky was just turning pink when command ordered all positions to "**ADVANCE!**"

Thus began another day of back and forth skirmishes. The Marines would drive the VC back then the VC would move forward a few yards. Nothing seemed to be changing the standoff.

It continued that way for the better part of the day. The advantage soon fell to the Marines when the Marine Command Center called for a **NAPALM STRIKE !**

When the 'Flowers of Hell'—as the VC called it—began to rain down on them, their resolve melted and they fled to escape cremation.

All that was left was to police up the area, gather up the dead and wounded form both sides. retrieve any weapons or ammunition which had survived the flames and di-di for Red Beach Base.

On the return ride the Marines and the entire photo team were silent. The day had evoked a new feeling of their limited mortality and they withdrew into their thoughts and memories of these last two days.

FOURTEEN

Red Beach Base was a welcome sight to the survivors of the days of heart-stopping battle and, as they piled out of the trucks and fell into formation, they noted the empty spots where their buddies had stood only days before.

There was no laughing or joking among the troops this day. It was a sad and solemn day.

As Chief Gilmore told the men when they returned to Barracks Five:

"You men can thank the Good Lord that we're still here. I'm not an outwardly religious man but I do believe in a higher Being and I, for one, will be saying a prayer of Thanks to Him for bringing us safely through this bloody day. And I'll also include a prayer for the men who gave all, today!"

"AMEN!"

When everyone had had a shower to wash off the grime of the jungle and had put on clean uniforms, the sound of the bugle calling **"ASSEMBLY"** called the troops to formation in front of the Command HQ.

There followed a solemn memorial service for the troops lost on the field of battle.

Seth had gotten permission from the CO to film the ceremony, promising a copy to the families of the dead.

"I know they'd appreciate that, Petty Officer, and thank you for offering," the CO said.

Following the services, all adjourned to the mess hall for the first hot meal in three days.

Baldy especially enjoyed the feed saying:

"My backbone was kissing my belly-button I was so hungry." he announced.

His feed didn't take long to digest as he soon found a pressing need to trot to the latrine.

"Chief," he said on his return from his urgent call of nature, "I think I caught a case of distemper. I barely made it to the throne before the dam busted."

"Baldy, I think you mean 'dysentery'. distemper is something a dog gets—but then you could be right, you dog-face. No tellin' what you might have come down with."

"OK, 'distemper' or 'dysentery', all I know is I got the 'Saigon Trots' and I need to stay close to the head or start wearing a diaper!"

Baldy's description of his malady produced gales of laughter from the team—even though he had their sympathy.

"Don't worry Baldy," Seth said between chuckles, "As the old saying goes: 'THIS TOO SHALL PASS!'"

Which brought forth even louder guffaws.

A day of bed-rest, plenty of fluids and a variety of pills soon had Baldy cured of his 'distemper'.

"Chief Gilmore," the Marine PAO, Captain Morgan said, "We have a medical aid facility here on base where we get a lot of casualties straight from the front and my CO wondered if you might have time to shoot some film on their operation before you go? They take care of getting the wounded stabilized fit to be transported over to the Da Nang Hospital and have saved many a wounded man's life by their quick attention."

"Captain, we will **make** time to give your medics the credit they so well deserve." the Chief replied enthusiastically.

"Incidentally," the Captain added, "Three of the 'Medics' are Navy Hospital Corpsmen on duty with our Marine Battalion. They're more than 'pill-pushers'. They get involved in much of the work in the operating room just as much as the two nurses we have in our Aid Station. They're 'A-number one' medical professionals and we're proud to call them "Marines'."

"Captain, I've served with many Navy Corpsmen in my 24 years in the Navy and I totally agree, they're the greatest! Just point us in the direction of your aid station and we'll get our cameras rollin'."

Helos were just arriving with wounded from another battle when the photo team walked into the OR prep-room.

"You men will need to wash up and get into sterile scrubs before entering the treatment room." one of the Navy medics instructed them, "We have two serious cases and four minor injuries, so you should have plenty of 'fodder' for your cameras. All we ask is don't get in the way and move when we say **'move'!**"

"You're the boss in there, Doc," Gilmore replied, "We've all done some shooting in the OR so we pretty much know our way around, but whatever you say is our command! I guarantee!"

"I hope none of you guys get 'queazy' at the sight of blood cause these things can get pretty gory at times."

"No sweat, Doc, as I said—been there, done that."

"OK, let's roll, then. They're wheelin' in the first man now."

It was a marvel to witness the teamwork and swift efficiency of the surgical staff. Every move was choreographed and conversation was limited to only what was required.

The photo crew exited the OR after all the wounded had been treated and either flown to Da Nang or sent to the aid station's six-bed recovery room to heal there patched up injuries.

"MAN," Roger commented, "Those medics are the greatest. If I ever—heaven forbid—get so much as a splinter I hope there's one of those guys around."

"They do nice work, alright," Louie agreed.

All that was left now was to add the aid station footage to their film package and head for Da Nang and a flight back to Ton San Nhut.

"Guys," the Chief said, "I want to hand you a BRAVO-ZULU (Well Done) for the way you came through on this one. All tolled, I think we all did a 'bang-up' job! CINCPAC should he mighty pleased when they view this production!"

"And it won't hurt that we got that extra coverage of medics treating the wounded, either," Seth added, "BUMED (Navy Bureau of Medicine and Surgery) will 'cream their jeans' over that stuff, you betchum."

"I think this ought to be worth at least two days of R&R in Saigon. Don't you Chief?" Baldy suggested.

No answer from the Chief and no disagreement from any of team.

As it turned, out a semblance of calm fell over the country. Only an occasional small skirmish interrupted the peace when patrols, from both sides encountered one another. The men of CCG ALPHA-TWO team took full advantage of the lull to catch up on rest, letter writing and just general goofing off.

The calm before the storm bothered the usually active men.

"Lt., One of the Da Nang corpsmen was telling me about a squad of Seabees in a small village, four or five clicks west of Saigon, who might be good for a story," Seth mentioned, "They're doing 'people-to-people' work with the inhabitants and having pretty good success.

"What really got him on the subject—next to the village the ARVN have a VC POW compound and the Seabee corpsman has volunteered his time and talent to hold 'sick-call' twice-a-week for the prisoners."

"Sounds good, Seth. Why don't you drive over there and check it out. I think I have another project that we ought to look into while we're all just sittin' on our butts. I've been hearing about something called 'Operation Marketplace' that the Navy is involved in. It's a fleet of sampans and small boats crewed by armed South Vietnamese former fishermen patrolling the coastal waters looking for gun-runners. The boats are skippered by US Navy officers who arrest and haul in any smugglers encountered."

"Lt., I'll take on that job," Louie volunteered.

"I'd like Baldy to go, too. That way you two can ride separate boats, the better to be there if they waylay any enemy craft."

"What have you got for me, Lt.?" Roger ask.

"I really don't have anything at the moment, Rog. Why don't you just stand by in case something comes up. You can spend some time with your fiancé in the mean time—I guess you don't mind that, do you?"

"Are you kiddin'. Lately I've been spending too much time away, and we got some 'makin' up' to do—and, Lt., you'll please note—I said 'makin' **UP!** not 'makin' **OUT!'**

"Believe it or not, Guys, we're still holding back until our wedding night!"

"And then, **look out for the fireworks!"** Baldy laughed.

Seth found the small hootch the Seabees called 'home' and informed the Petty Officer in charge of his plan to document their work.

"I'm Bos'n's Mate First Larry Olson, and we're happy to have you aboard, Seth. I hope you can find enough material here to make it worth your drive up here."

"I've been informed that your work with the village people has been pretty impressive," Seth corrected Petty Officer Olson, "and the story about your corpsman and the POWs is more than worth my trip."

"Well, you'll have to wait 'til morning to catch our hospital corpsman at work with the POWs. He holds 'sick call' for them twice a week at 0900 and you're in luck, tomorrow's his next scheduled visit. I'll have to clear you with the ARVN prison warden. You'll be going inside the compound so all visitors have to have approval before entering. It shouldn't be a problem though. We have a very cooperative agreement. It's just a formality. You understand?"

"Sure, I understand that, Larry, and I need to let my CO know that I'll be staying over. He expected this to only take a day. I know it will be no problem, but, I should clue him in."

"We have field-phone contact with COMNAVFORV so we'll have them pass the word to your unit."

Seth occupied the rest of the day with following the Seabee personnel around the village doing odd jobs for the Vietnamese residents. A thatch roof repair here, renewing rock-work on a cooking fire-pit, filling in potholes (mainly shell craters), installing a replacement pump on the village's only well.

Seth also learned that one of the men was helping a Vietnamese girl teach some of the village children basic arithmetic and English.

"I definitely want to do something with that, too," he told Olson.

"He'll be holding classes this evening, over in the mess tent. I hope you brought flash equipment with you. We don't have any electricity so we can't provide you with anything but a few Coleman™ lanterns."

"I only brought one little pocket flash with me as I didn't expect to do any night shooting. I'll just have to boost the ASA of my Tri-X and mark the film for 'special processing'. We'll figure something out. I've had worse obstacles to overcome in this tour."

The rest of Seth's day went smoothly and he managed to get interviews and pix of all the Seabees in the unit before adjourning for evening chow.

Evening meal over, the tent was cleared and Seth and the Seabee volunteer 'school master' set up the makeshift classroom in one corner of the mess tent. When Seth began setting up the lanterns to light the instructors and students (all five of them) he found he still had insufficient light for decent exposure. Even after recalculating the sensitivity of his Tri-X by a factor of four, there still wasn't enough light.

"I've an idea we might try," he remarked, "In earlier days, I saw an old Mickey Rooney movie where he was portraying the life of Thomas Edison and, in one scene, a doctor was going to have to operate under adverse light conditions. Well Edison (Mickey) had them bring in a bureau with a big mirror. And pushed it close to the table and put the lamps in front of the mirror. With the combined light from the lamps and the reflected light from the mirror illuminating the scene he had increased the total candlepower to more than double the output of the lamps alone. Can you rustle up a large, mirror, maybe 3'x4' or 4'x6' and let's see if it works?"

"Hot damn, Seth, you just might have hit on an answer to the problem,"

The CB soon returned carrying, with the help of another CB, a large mirror suitable for the need.

With the mirror and four lanterns in place Seth let out a **"WHOOP!"**

"My meter shows we're just under 'the wire'," he reported, ***"Thank God for Movie Trivia!"*** he shouted.

The problem solved, Seth proceeded to document the five students and the two instructors in their make-do classroom.

"This story ought to be Pulitzer material if they give any credit for overcoming adversity," the CB instructor commented.

"Well, maybe not 'Pulitzer', but sure enough Front Page!" agreed Seth.

That night Seth slept peacefully with the satisfaction of having done a good day's work. He awoke in the morning ready to tackle the POW story, knowing that it would be anti-climatic after last night's accomplishment.

At 0900 Seth and HM Third Class Jack Tyler were ushered through the prison security gate and the corpsman began laying out his medical supplies.

"I get everything here from an intestinal problem to a cut or bruise and even, once a boil on the butt of a fifty-year-old man. He had a little 'fu manchu' goatee which bobbled up and down as he tried to thank me," Tyler told Seth, "If an inmate's condition is too serious, I call in medical transport and the prisoner is taken to the Da Nang Hospital. Most times, though, their ailments are simple where a pill or a band-aid does the trick."

Corpsman Tyler had been given the name 'Bac Si' (Doc) by the grateful prisoners, and had earned their friendship and respect.

By 1030 all the filming of the ailing prisoners had been competed, the last patient treated and Seth thanked the Seabees for their great cooperation. Now he was ready to hit the road back to Ton San Nhut, with what he knew to be one of his better efforts.

Louie and Baldy had hitched a ride down to Na Bey and boarded a couple of "Operation Market Place' boats preparing to go out on patrol. The boats were modified Vietnamese fishing boars rigged with two 100 HP Evinrude motors that could outrun most of the craft operated by the Communist smugglers.

The Lt. skippering the boat Louie had picked, was from a family of North Pacific fishermen and could handle his craft like he was riding a motorcycle. He was called 'Lieutenant Hornet' by his Vietnamese crew. His real name being 'Horn**er**' but his men say 'he sting like a bee' so he was named '**Hornet!'**

Baldys' Navy skipper was just as colorful as Lt 'Hornet' but with the simple name of 'Ted'.

His crew had a saying about him though: "You f—ck with Lt. Ted, you **DEAD!"**

In both boat crews there was a strong bond of camaraderie. It was almost like a three musketeers 'one for all and all for one' sort of accord.

Both boats got under way and headed down-stream to the open waters of the South China Sea. Today the water was as smooth as glass and the boats skimmed along at moderate speed. All hands were on high alert looking for signs of any other craft on the water. For over an hour they cruised up and down the coast searching the surface.

One of the Vietnamese sailors, through the on-board interpreter, informed Lt. Horner he'd spotted a craft on the horizon off the starboard bow.

The Lt. quickly swung the boat right and accelerated to top speed. The target boat attempted to take evasive action but quickly realized the futility of trying to get away from the powerful pursuing craft so hove-to and cut their engine.

The boat appeared to be a simple fishing craft and the occupants didn't seem to be armed so the Lt. pulled alongside and tossed a line indicating they should tie up the boats. Three of Lt. Horner's crew went aboard and proceeded to search for any contraband or weapons but found nothing but a meager day's fishing catch. With apologies and a couple cartons of cigarettes the lines were thrown off and both boats went their separate ways.

Baldy's boat had idled their motors and stood off until the all clear signal had been given. They were prepared to swing around to the opposite side of the fishing boat if any resistance was forthcoming and provide fire support.

"Some days it's like this and other days we catch a boat with smugglers and they have to be subdued, captured or killed," Lt. Ted said.

The two boats continued patrolling the off-shore Vietnam waters and came up with no further encounters for the remainder of the day.

"I guess we have to go with the pix we got," Louie complained, "But we did come up with enough to give the homefolks an idea of the 'Market Place' mission.

"Thanks for the boat ride, Lt., Maybe we can do this again some time. Best of luck to you and your crews."

FIFTEEN

"Guys," Lt. Crocket addressed the Team, "Our relief team is getting formed up in 'Diego and it looks like there'll be some changes in personnel. Senior Chief Brady, who headed up Team Alpha-One, has been promoted to **Master** Chief and is being transferred to the Office of Chief of Naval Information in DC to run the Still Section desk.

"A.J. Jameson got his chief's hat by way of a 'Ho Chi Minh' advancement and will lead the new team. The rest of CCG Team Alpha-One have been shuffled around so I'm not sure who will be making up the balance of 'A.J.'s team.

"They aren't due in 'Nam' for three more weeks so you have plenty of time to get all your 'Action Reports' and other paper-work brought up to date. Any time you aren't deployed on a job, I want you guys to work on having this place ready to turn over to them so they can step right in and take over."

"**THREE WEEKS?**" cried Louie, "That'll be like an eternity!"

"Not if you keep your ass occupied with **work**, lil' Buddy," Chief Gilmore chided him. "time flies when your having fun—so just have fun with your work!"

And 'work' they did! With two extra typewriters borrowed from the 7th Fleet yeomen, the paperwork was attacked and dealt with in short order. The 'Action Reports' required a bit of consultation among the men to get the dates and locations of their projects correct. Duplicates of all the data sheets that had been submitted with the film shipped were correlated and put in time and date order.

"You Guys really buckled down and cleared up all this paperwork in 'jig' time," the Lt. complimented, "I think we damn near got the 'turnover' details whipped. Take some time now to get all your personal matters in order. Make sure you all get your 'going home' shots, pay vouchers prepared and any other matters taken care of. I'll set it up with the Army Hospital here to schedule the shots."

"Crap, Lt. do we have to get stuck with a bunch of needles before we're through with this 'hell away from home'?" Baldy complained.

"Absolutely! The Navy doesn't want you carrying any Vietnamese germs—like dengue fever, malaria, hepatitis and who knows what else—back with you to spread around among the home-folks."

"I've had one of those hepatitis shots before, and believe me, it's like getting stabbed in the keester with a red-hot six-penny nail!" added Louie.

"It's regulations, so all hands will comply! I'll put out the word when we're scheduled."

The notice went out to all troops that a large segment of the foliage along the Saigon river had been sprayed with 'Agent Orange' and all personnel were to stay clear of the area for the next two days.

"It isn't known what the effect would be on humans but we can't take any chances," the 7th Fleet Operations Officer warned the men, "It's meant to kill off most of the undergrowth and bushes to remove cover for the enemy, but it could also be harmful to humans and animals. So, just head the warning and 'don't go near the water'! Give the sh—t time to clear."

"Now we got that to worry about! What's next?" Roger asked.

Next day, Lt. Crocket, announced that the dreaded shots were scheduled for 1000 AM.

"All hands will be mustered at the Hospital so don't any of you sh—t birds try to skip out!"

The shots were given expertly by the Army Nurse and no one complained about pain—until it came to the gamma globulin shot for hepatitis—. It was just as Louie had described and all hands went away with an aversion to sitting down for a couple of hours.

"I didn't mind baring my butt for that pretty nurse but, when she hit me with that hot poker, I jumped a foot." Brady told the men, "I came damn close to running out of that Hospital with my pants still wrapped around my ankles!"

"That would've been a sight to see," Roger laughed, "I can just picture him running down Tu Do Street. His hairy ass and legs bared for all the world to ogle."

"'tain't funny Magee!"

When night came all hands turned in for a good night's shut-eye. But, it didn't last long! Around one AM their slumber was brought to a sudden halt.

"UP AND AT 'EM! GANG. WE GOT TROUBLE IN RIVER CITY!" Lt. Crocket yelled, "The Mandarin Hotel just down the street has been car-bombed—or I should say—pedi-cab bombed!

"**HOLY SH—,**" Seth exclaimed, "That's an enlisted billeting hotel!"

"CINCPAC Operations Officer is in a jeep at the gate with an Army MP and a Cahn Sat Officer (City Police) waiting to give us an escort to the fire.

"Everybody grab your cameras and vests we got work to do!"

"How'd it happen?" the Chief inquired, as they sped through the congested emergency traffic.

"Some 'Dink' sneaked into the alley next to the hotel and left his pedi-cab parked there loaded with C-4," the MP informed the men, "He proceeded to make tracks down the street just as the charge detonated, blowing a hole in the side of the hotel a tank could drive through.

"It was just dumb luck that he picked that spot to set it off. The major damage was to the kitchen and the ballroom which were on that side of the building. There were some casualties on the second floor above the kitchen but we can't be sure how bad it is until they get the fire put out and can get inside and clear the rubble.

"Another security team saw the bomber running down the dark street, seconds before the blast, and had apprehended him for violation of curfew."

"I guess that was another 'dumb' move," Louie said, "Not thinking; about the curfew patrols. If the 'White Mice' (Cahn Sat cops) took custody of him, his ass is grass. They're a tough bunch and don't treat their prisoners with 'kid gloves'! If they had been aware he had just set off that bomb, he'd be dead meat by now."

The cameramen were kept busy for 2 ½ hours filming the destruction from every angle. Louie, in his enthusiasm for that perfect shot, was forcibly dragged out of the kitchen area by one of the Navy firefighters.

"We don't need no more 'crispy critters' if one of those burning beams happen to drop on your head, Sailor!" the fireman admonished him.

"Sorry, Mate. Just got a little carried away!"

"You'll get carried away, alright, feet first, if you ain't careful, fella!"

As the flames were gradually brought under control, Navy investigators began the dirty job of sifting through the ashes for evidence and, heaven forbid, casualties. Every little bit of evidence, and every charred bit of structure had to be photographed and logged. This kept the CCG team hopping to get the pix and record it's significance for future examination when a Military Inquiry is convened. It was such a chore that the Lt. ordered Seth to sheath his camera and do the picture logging for the others.

"We can't afford to screw up any of these shots because we miss-captioned them."

Seth was able to simplify his job by using his pocket-recorder to dictate the needed information which he could later transcribe.

"Great idea," Gilmore complimented him.

"That handy-dandy Sony™ is my handiest tool when it comes to doing my stories," Seth chuckled, "No reason why it ain't just as valuable in this case."

A grimy, soot covered bunch finally returned to their Villa, just as the sun was peeking over the Saigon roof-tops. The single shower in the Villa got a workout as the soiled men tried to crowd more than one man at a time into the small stall.

"KEEP YOUR MITTS TO YOURSELVES, GUYS !!" someone in the tangle of bodies hollered.

"Soap down—step out and scrub—get back in—and rinse! That's the Navy Way!" the Chief directed.

"It's when I'm soapin' and rinsing' that I think somebody's trying to 'cop a feel'," Louie answered, "I hope we head home soon, 'cause I think some of these characters are getting too horny."

"My advice to you 'studs' is, keep you pants zippered and your legs crossed," Chief Gilmore warned, "At this late date you don't want to catch something you wouldn't want to take home to your wife or best girl. Take it from a guy who's been deployed away from home tak-san times, 'abstinence makes the heart grow fonder'!"

"That ain't gonna' be easy, Chief," Baldy said, "Every day it gets harder!"

"And **harder**," Louie added with a cackle at his off-the-cuff, off-color pun.

"When you guys get the crud washed off, and your minds out of the gutter, hit the sack, and try to get some rest!" the Chief ordered, "Ain't no telling' how long it'll be before we have to mount up again!"

Thirty-six hours passed before the team was requested to 'mount up'. By that time, they had rested and were getting 'ant-sy' for new adventures. The team was assembled in the Tan Son Nhut Office awaiting Lt. Crocket's return from 7th Fleet's morning briefing.

"What 'ya got for us today, Lt.?" Seth inquired.

"It seems they want some more coverage of the SEAL teams' intel gathering operations," he replied, "I want two volunteers to hook-up with the SEALs down in Na Bay and go along on one of their missions. This will be another stealth job and they'll be avoiding any engagement, if possible.

"Just be prepared if that ain't 'possible' though!"

"I'll go on this one, Lt," Roger spoke up.

"Me too!" Louie added.

"OK, then. That's settled. "You other three will make another visit to the Cam Ranh Bay construction site for some up-date stuff on the progress. I don't expect you'll run into any action, as they've opened up a new road and it's moderately secure. Just stay safe—all of you!"

"Saddle-up, cowboys. We're off to the Vietnam Rodeo!" Gilmore ordered.

The next morning, bright and early, both crews were loaded up and moving out. Roger and Louie would lay over in the SEAL barge until nightfall when the team would embark on their intelligence-gathering jaunt. The three photographers going to Cam Ranh Bay piled their gear into the van and hit the road at first light.

As the Lt. had informed them, their trip to Cam Ranh Bay was smooth over the new road and no incidents occurred on the way. They were greeted by a completely changed landscape when they arrived. Dozens of buildings and warehouses were now standing where, before, only piles of sand and materials had covered the site.

"Boy! These guys've sure been busy," Seth commented, "Between the 'Can-Do' Seabees and the civilian contractor, they've turned this sand-pile into a city, almost overnight."

"WOW!' was the only utterance from Baldy.

They checked in with Lt. Maloney, the Seabee they'd worked with previously and were greeted with:

"Welcome back, Guys. How d'ya like our new digs? A bit of an improvement from a few weeks ago when you were here, huh?

"We have a new Butler-Hut barracks, and mess-hall, a new All-Hands Club and lounge, machinery shops. Name it we got it! We also have half-a-dozen warehouses down by the new pier. "We're 'bout ready to dedicate the place and go into business!"

"I can tell you're proud of the job—and WELL YOU SHOULD BE!" the Chief enthusiastically replied. "We'll unpack our gear and get our cameras rollin'," he said, "We got a lot of sh—t to cover, so we best hump it!"

In short order, the three photogs separated and began filming everything in sight.

"Make sure you get plenty of establishing shots, and every angle you can to show off the improvements they've made. Don't spare the film!" Chief Gilmore told the men Baldy managed to get some 'artsy-fartsy' shots of the warehouses and piers in silhouette against the crimson sunset.

"DC will love that stuff, for sure!" he bragged.

"Knock off for tonight," Gilmore said, "We'll be back out here tomorrow and giv'er Hell."

Roger and Louie were quietly cruising down into the Delta with the SEALs. This was a 'stealth' mission, so there was no chatter. Only the slight hum of the powerful electric motor propelling them further into the swamp. The jungle noises were the only other sounds breaking the stillness. All communication among the men was by hand signals only.

It was so quiet, Baldy later claimed, he could hear Louie's heart beating on the other side of the boat.

Forty minutes up the small stream, the SEAL team leader signaled to pull the boat over to the bank and all silently slipped into the brush. Thorns and sharp edged palmetto fronds snatched at their clothes and scratched their skin wherever it was not protected. The hike continued for over an hour when the point man signaled to ***"halt"***. Through the dense underbrush was visible a thatch hut. There was a small fire just outside the doorway which partially illuminate two men sitting to the side smoking their pipes and conversing in subdued tones.

The SEAL leader signaled three of his men to sneak around the back of the hut and flank the two Vietnamese. Two more SEALs were directed to crawl as close as they could to the men and silently throttle them before they could react. No other VC were visible, if there were any more in the area, but the other two SEALs were placed with their backs facing the hut to cover the rear, just in case.

In one coordinated move the two men near the fire were put out of action and the lead SEAL stealthily entered the hut and gathered up any papers which might reveal location or movement of any VC forces. That accomplished, the signal was given to pull back and return to the boat.

Back on the boat and proceeding back down the river, the lead SEAL was busily examining, by flashlight, the seized paperwork.

"From what I can decipher from this stuff, we got what we came for!" he whispered. Then gave the signal to hit full speed and get back to base.

Because of the need for silence, Roger and Louie were not able to do any filming on the way in, but, when the SEALs attacked the two smokers they both rolled their cameras and, by the light of the fire, got a good record of the action.

The jungle began to grow lighter with the imminent sunrise, so Roger and Louie were able to get some more on-board shots. Because of the SEAL policy of not exposing the men's identity, they had to use caution to get them only in silhouette or from the rear. Still, the two photographers felt that they had done a good job of documenting the SEALs' covert mission.

"I sure hope this is our last foray I into those swamps," Louie said, "I get the 'heeby-jeebys' every time I look up at the tops of those palms. I keep seeing a 'dink' sniper up there putting me in his sights!"

"You ain't alone in thinking' that," Roger affirmed Louie's words.

A brief, but bumpy jeep ride back to Ton San Nhut and the two could let down their guard and relax over a beer at the Club with the rest of the team.

Final preparations began for the 'turn-over' in one week. PHC A. J. Jameson and his new CCG Team Alpha-One was due to arrive in three days.

"We gotta' throw a shindig when they git here," Baldy suggested, "A welcome aboard party for them and a 'Goombey' party for **US**!"

"You're always ready to party at the drop of a 'pop-top', Baldy," Seth said, "But I agree this time! After six months in this 'Pearl of the Orient' we all deserve a bang-up, kick up your heels, send off!"

"Louie. You're in charge of the vittles." ordered the Lt., "Use your contacts at the docks and rustle some steaks and all the trimmin's. Just don't get caught doing that scroungin' that you do so well! We want you to be on that US-bound plane with us, when we kiss Tan Son Nhut **'GOODBY'!**"

Three days later, Chief A.J. Jameson and his four-man Alpha-One crew arrived from Tachikawa Air Base in the early afternoon. Seth met them at the Tan Son Nhut terminal with the van and carted them and their gear over to the Office where Team Alpha-Two was gathered to greet them.

There followed a melee of hand-shaking, hugging and joyful pats on the back. Everyone tried to talk at once, until Lt. Crocket silenced them with a loud whistle.

"OK. Everyone calm down. As is obvious, Chief Jameson, this bunch of 'lean-hard-jungle-Fighters' are glad to see you made it! They're all about 'psycho' and could go 'NUTS' any minute!"

"Lt.," A.J. answered, "I remember the feeling. I hope SENIOR Chief Gilmore gets them home in time!—YES, I said **'SENIOR'** Chief! I was ordered to deliver this 'Certificate Of Appointment to the Rate of Senior Chief' directly to Chief Gilmore immediately on arriving here.

"I present you with your new insignia of 'Fouled Anchor with Star'. Congratulations, SENIOR CHIEF. When the Command found out you turned down a medal for your heroic charge against the enemy-attack, Washington approved your advancement. YOU"VE MORE THAN EARNED IT !"

"HOLY CATS !" Baldy shouted, "THIS REALLY CALLS FOR A **PARTY !!**"

And a **!! PARTY !!** was had! And **WHAT A PARTY IT WAS!** Two days later, when CCG Team Alpha-Two boarded the PANAM flight, extra doses of aspirin were needed to soothe the still painful hangovers.—For all but Roger!

He had skipped the party to make sure the papers were all signed and notarized for his fiancé to be allowed to be on the same flight. He and Xuan (Anne) didn't want any foul ups to delay their wedding plans upon arrival in Michigan. Abstinence all these months had tried their pledge to the limits.

Excitement was running high and, as the aircraft picked up it's wheels, a deafening cheer drowned out the sound of the four jet engines

"HOORAH!"

AUTHOR'S EPILOGUE

Writing this novel and the preceding one—*"Those Crazy Camera Guys'*—has been a dream fulfilled. For months after my return from my final tour in Vietnam, I was bothered by the stories I was reading in books, magazines and news media and seeing in movies and TV about how 'terrible our men had performed'. These were exaggerations and applied to a very small number of men.

I had seen a different side of that unnecessary conflict. It came to a point where my wife, Eva, to whom I dedicated *"Those Crazy Camera Guys"* advised me:

"Stop complaining about it! You should write a book telling the other stories about serving in Vietnam."

The results of putting it on paper was cathartic and allowed me to clear my mind of the memories—good and bad—that I had suppressed for almost four decades.

Both of these novels are 95% fiction and 5% biographical.

My thanks to my wife for her inspiration and for urging me to write these novels.

K.